Make
Your Own
Fishing Lures

Also by Vlad Evanoff:

Surf Fishing
Fishing Secrets of the Experts
Fresh-Water Fisherman's Bible
1001 Fishing Tips and Tricks
Another 1001 Fishing Tips and Tricks
Complete Guide to Fishing
How To Fish in Salt Water
Modern Fishing Tackle
Spin Fishing

MAKE
YOUR OWN
FISHING LURES

Vlad Evanoff

SOUTH BRUNSWICK AND NEW YORK: A. S. BARNES AND COMPANY
LONDON: THOMAS YOSELOFF LTD

© 1975 by A. S. Barnes and Co., Inc.

A. S. Barnes and Co., Inc.
Cranbury, New Jersey 08512

Thomas Yoseloff Ltd
108 New Bond Street
London W1Y OQX, England

Library of Congress Cataloging in Publication Data

Evanoff, Vlad.
    Make your own fishing lures.

    Includes index.
    1. Fishing lures. I. Title.
SH449.E9 1975   688.7′9   74-14259
ISBN 0-498-01617-X

PRINTED IN THE UNITED STATES OF AMERICA

CONTENTS

PREFACE

One of the most satisfying experiences a fisherman can have is to catch a fish on a fishing lure that he has fashioned with his own hands. The trout angler has excellent books on how to tie his own flies, but little printed information has been available to anglers who want to make their own plugs, spoons, spinners, metal squids, jigs, plastic worms, tube lures, and other fresh and saltwater lures. So that is how this book came to be written.

As these pages will demonstrate it is not necessary to be a skilled craftsman to make lures. Most anglers already possess the ability to handle the few necessary tools, and if they follow the directions and also let the illustrations guide them, they can make good lures. They may not be professionally perfect, but they will catch fish, and that's all that really counts.

And if the angler makes his own lures, he'll probably catch more fish, in the long run. The reason for this is psychological. An angler who uses a store-bought plug or jig tends to be hesitant about casting around rocks, logs, piles, and masses of weeds. He figures that he paid good money for it and doesn't want to lose it—even though he knows some of the best fish are caught around such obstructions. And some lures such as jigs are more effective when bounced on the bottom or trolled deep, where they often get fouled and lost. So rather than lose his costly lures our cautious angler casts into safer spots, which contain fewer fish!

The angler who makes his own lures just doesn't have such inhibitions. He figures that the lure he ties to his line cost him very little in cold cash and was easy and fun to make. So what, if it gets lost? He casts into all kinds of risky spots and loses some lures. He also catches more than his share of fish. Another reason for making your own lures is that the angler who buys his lures in a store usually carries one or two of a certain type or size. If he loses them, he's through fishing for the day, if the fish happen to want that particu-

lar lure. But the make-them-yourself angler usually carries plenty of
spares and rarely runs short.

Making fishing lures can be an enjoyable hobby, especially during the long winter months when fishing is slow. It has even been
argued that the joy of designing and creating a lure offers as much
if not more pleasure than the actual fishing itself!

So, have fun! Good luck and good fishing with your own lures.

Make
Your Own
Fishing Lures

1

TOOLS

Before you can make any kind of fishing lures you must have the proper tools. In fact, without the right tools you can't do a good job, and you'll soon become discouraged. On the other hand, if you are equipped with the right tools you'll find lure-making easy and highly enjoyable. So the best procedure is to obtain as many of the necessary tools in advance before you start making your own lures.

Most anglers will already have some of the tools described here. The rest can be bought without too much of an investment, and the others can be acquired as the need arises for them. Unless you want to make all the lures in this book, you won't need every single tool listed here. If you read the chapter on the particular lure or lures you want to make, you'll get a good idea of the tools you'll need. Then make a list of the tools that will be needed to make those lures. Naturally, many of the same tools will be used for most of the fishing lures, but some lures will require special tools that must be bought or obtained.

The biggest single item needed for making fishing lures is a bench, table, or desk. Fortunate, indeed, is the man who has a basement, den, or special room where he can have a permanent workbench and various power tools to pursue his hobbies. For many this is out of the question, and they have to do their work on a kitchen table or desk that must also serve for other uses. This tends to discourage many who are irked by the chore of taking out and putting away tools and materials every time they want to work on fishing lures. If you have no permanent workbench the best solution is to keep your tools and lure-making materials in a chest, cabinet, or drawer where they are available quickly.

After you have such a bench, table, or desk you need a vise (Fig.

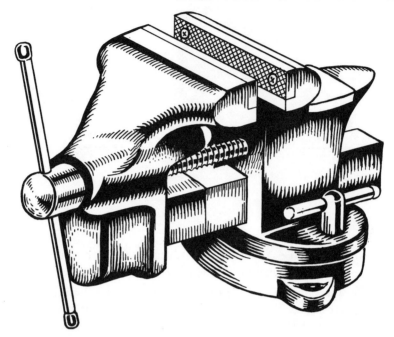

Figure A.

Bench vise.

A) that will hold the various lures for drilling, filing, bending, and other operations. Almost any bench vise of good size will serve the purpose. Unless you have a permanent workbench, this vise doesn't have to be fastened to the table or desk until it is needed.

A small anvil is also useful if you plan to make many metal lures or parts for such lures. It is used for cutting, bending, punching, and riveting. However, if you get a big bench vise of the machinist's or utility type you can use the anvil surface found on such vises. Or you can obtain a small block of iron with a smooth surface to use as a makeshift anvil.

A hammer, of course, is a basic tool for any kind of work, and for making fishing lures about two or three hammers will be enough. If you already have a claw hammer (Fig. B), you can use it for many lure-making jobs. However, you should also get at least one ball peen or machinist's hammer that can be used for shaping metal, driving punches, cold chisels, and other uses. A twelve-ounce ball peen hammer is a good size for all-around work. Another type of hammer that is good to have is a soft-faced hammer. These are made of plastic or have rawhide, fiber, or lead faces. The soft-faced

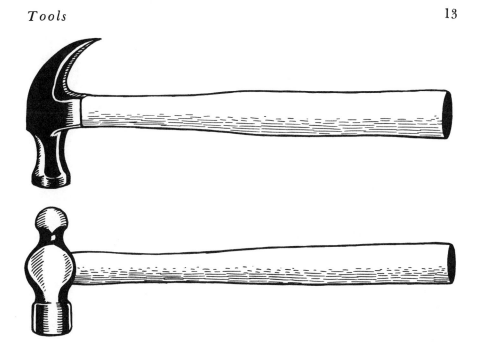

Figure B.   *Claw hammer (above) and ball peen hammer.*

hammer is used for bending and shaping metal and leaves no tool marks. A wooden mallet (Fig. C) is also needed if you plan to shape your own metal spoons or spinners.

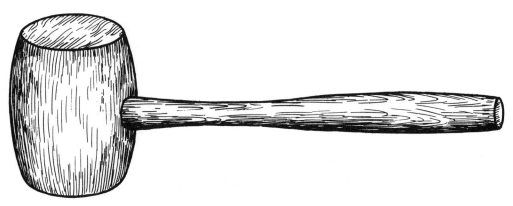

Wooden mallet.   *Figure C.*

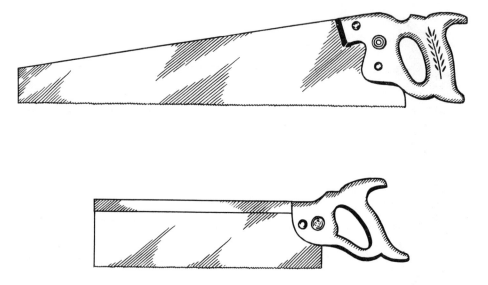

Hand saw (above) and back saw.   *Figure D.*

About three saws will be needed. If you already have a hand saw (Fig. D) it can be used for working with wood. Since most fishing lures are small, however, a back saw that has a thin blade and fine teeth is even better than a large hand saw with coarse teeth for accurate cutting. The other saw that is needed is a hacksaw (Fig. E), which is needed for cutting metal and other hard materials such as plastics. There are many types of hacksaws on the market, but the adjustable frame type with a pistol grip is best. You will also need several kinds of blades to use with the hacksaw. These blades have from fourteen to thirty-two teeth to the inch and come in all-hard or flexible tempers. Each type is best for a certain job, depending on the metal or material you are cutting. If you have one or two blades of each kind you'll be prepared for any cutting job.

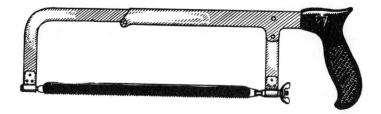

Figure E.   *Hacksaw.*

Some kind of drill is needed for drilling holes in wood and metal. If you have a home workshop with a drill press you can use it for most of the work to be done. It is especially useful when drilling holes in metal. A portable electric drill (Fig. F) is also a big aid when drilling metal, especially if you have to drill many holes. It can also be used with all kinds of burrs, bits, and grinders for shaping or hollowing out wooden lures such as plugs. Most of the drilling will be done in wood or softer metals such as brass and copper or aluminum. Here an ordinary hand drill (Fig. G) will serve the purpose. Such a hand drill will usually take drills up to ¼ inch in diameter. When buying a hand drill it's a good idea to get the best one you can afford. A cheap hand drill will soon break or wear out or not perform properly.

You also need a set of twist drills to use with an electric or hand drill. For the drill press or electric drill you will need a set of high-speed drills. The high-speed drills can be used for fast drilling without losing their temper. For drilling wood or soft metals carbon drills, which are cheaper than high-speed drills, can be used. You should get a complete set of drills up to about ¼ inch in diameter.

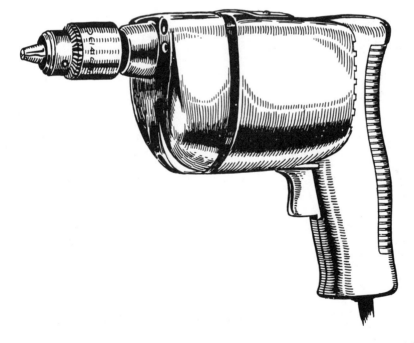

Figure F.   *Portable electric drill.*

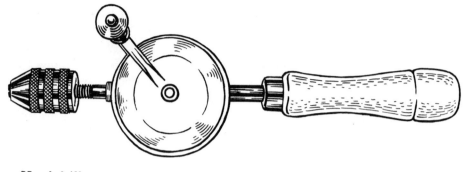

Hand drill.   *Figure G.*

The smaller sizes are the ones you will use most often. It's a good idea to buy two or three twist drills of the same size in the smaller sizes so that if you break one you'll have a spare.

A set of different kinds of pliers (Fig. H) is needed for many jobs encountered in making fishing lures. Combination pliers that have a slip joint that permits the jaws to open wide at the hinge to grip large diameters are useful for holding and bending metal.

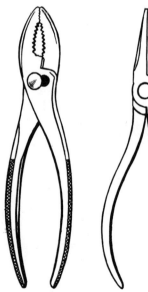

COMBINATION   FLAT NOSE   ROUND NOSE   DIAGONAL

Types of pliers.   *Figure H.*

Flat-nose pliers are also useful for holding or bending thin sheet metal or wire. They have a flat gripping surface between the jaws that will hold thin metal or wire firmly without damaging it too much.

Round-nosed pliers are needed for bending wire into various curves and eyes. They are especially useful in making spinner shafts and wire leaders. Both jaws of these pliers are round and tapered toward the end. Curves or eyes of small radius are bent with the tips of the jaws, while those of greater radius are bent with the base of the jaws. Even so, you'll need two or three pairs of round-nosed pliers in different sizes to handle most of the work. One pair can be the regular size used for heavy work, another a medium size, while the third can be the smaller jeweler-size round-nosed pliers. These can be used for making small curves or eyes and for fine wire.

Diagonal cutting pliers are used for cutting wire, nails, pins, and screws. The angle of the jaws on these pliers makes it possible to cut close to a surface. These pliers are designed for cutting mostly the softer metals and wire. However, they can be used for steel piano or stainless steel wire if they have very hard cutting jaws or edges. Because of this you should buy the best diagonal pliers you can get. Cheap ones will not do a good cutting job and the edges of the jaws will soon get nicked and ruined if used on hard wire.

For cutting sheet metal into various shapes you'll need hand snips (Fig. I). Although a pair of straight snips can be used both for straight cutting and for large curves, duckbill snips are more suitable for all-around work. The duckbill snips will cut straight edges or curves in either direction. These hand snips do not provide too much leverage and cutting thick metal is difficult. If you want to make it easier, you can get aviation metal snips, which have a compound lever action. They will cut thicker metal with much less effort.

You will also need an assortment of files to use on wood and metal. Files can be used to shape wooden fishing lures, for finishing metal molds, jigs, and other lures, for cutting tempered steel wire, hooks, and metal hardware, and for finishing metal lips, propellers, spinners, and spoons. Files are also needed to keep other tools sharp and in proper working order.

There are many different types of files in use but four kinds will take care of most of your needs (Fig. J). The flat file is one of the fastest cutting general-purpose files you can use. It has a broad surface and removes wood or metal quickly. You should get three flat files with different cuts. One should be a fine, single cut, which is used when a smooth finish is required. Another flat file should be a

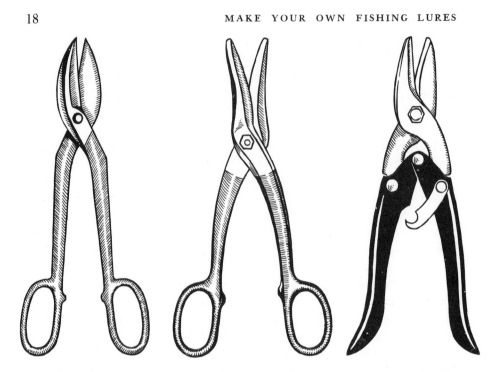

STRAIGHT   **DUCK BILL**   **AVIATION**

Figure I.   *Hand snips.*

FLAT   **ROUND**

TRIANGULAR   **HALF ROUND**

Shapes of files.   *Figure J.*

double-cut type, which is used for removing metal at a faster rate. This file leaves a rough surface that must be finished with a smooth file. The other type of flat file should be a rasp, which is used for rough work when you want to remove a lot of wood.

Still another file you need is a half-round file, which is also a good general-purpose tool. It has a flat face for flat filing and a curved side for filing grooves or round edges. This file can be obtained in different grades of coarseness.

A triangular or three-square file is used for filing metal smooth where small surfaces or corners must be worked. It can also be used to cut through heavy wire, rods, fishhooks, and other metal that cannot be cut with ordinary pliers. The triangular file is also handy for sharpening chisels, knives, and other cutting edges.

The round file or "rattail" file as the name implies is round and tapered toward the end. It is used to enlarge holes and to file half-round curves of small diameter.

You'll also need an assortment of screwdrivers of various lengths and blades. The standard screwdriver with a handle, shank, and blade will be the one mostly used and should be obtained in the smaller sizes. You rarely use big screws when making fishing lures, so the smaller screwdrivers will be needed most of the time.

The screws used in making lures are either plain or nickel-plated round-head brass screws. The sizes mostly used are No. 1 by 3/8 inch, No. 2 by 3/8 inch, No. 2 by 1/2 inch, and No. 2 by 5/8 inch. They should be made of brass because iron screws even if plated soon rust and weaken the wood, then pull out.

An electric soldering iron will be required for some jobs. Soldering irons come in various sizes, but the 90- or 100-watt iron is a good general-purpose type (Fig. K). With this, of course, you'll need soft solders that are alloys of lead and tin. They can be obtained in wire, ribbon, or bar form. The wire solder is the most convenient since it has a hollow core like a tube that contains a flux. If you use bar solder you'll have to buy a flux such as rosin or soldering paste. This is used to remove the oxide coating from metals so that the solder will take.

Figure K.   *Electric soldering iron.*

Then we have the various punches often needed when making fishing lures (Fig. L). The most useful is the center punch, which is used to make a mark on metal showing where to drill. For drilling wood you can use an ordinary ice pick or awl to make a starting hole. But for metal you need the center punch, which is struck with a hammer to make such an indentation. These punches come in various diameters and tapers, and two or three sizes will handle most jobs. Another handy punch is a starting punch, which has a long, gradual taper and a blunt point. This is used for clearing holes and can also be used to open the eyes on big hooks or screw eyes.

Center punch (above) and starting punch.   *Figure L.*

You should also possess at least one flat, cold chisel, which is used for cutting sheet metal, lead, tin, and other metals where other cutting tools cannot be used.

Finally, you need a sharp knife or two, single-edge razor blade, scissors, dividers, calipers, and a metal rule.

If you really plan to go into making wooden plugs seriously you'll find a wood- or metal-turning lathe invaluable for turning down such lures. Of course, this is quite an investment, and unless you really plan to make many fishing plugs it doesn't pay to buy a lathe for this purpose alone. But if you already have one you can use it for such work.

Somewhat less expensive but very handy is one of those hobby motorized tools that holds a large variety of small rotary tools. It can be used for drilling, grinding, polishing, carving, and other jobs. This tool is especially useful for finishing off metal molds.

When whittling or shaping wooden plugs or other lures by hand you'll find a set of wood-carving tools very useful. These have small, chisel-type blades that can be used to cut grooves, cups, holes, and similar indentations. The gouges that are part of these tools are especially useful for this work.

Then there are the various materials such as wood, metal, paints, lacquers, varnishes, hooks, screw eyes, wire, and other fishing-lure parts that you will need. These will be described in the following chapters in detail as the need arises for them. They can usually be bought in hardware stores, fishing tackle stores, or from mail-order houses. Mail-order houses often carry a large stock of fishing-lure parts. You'll find their addresses in the back of this book. Write for their catalogues to get descriptions of the lure parts with prices.

2

FRESHWATER PLUGS

The lure known as a *plug* had its origins in the distant past, and no one is sure who made the first lure for freshwater fishing. The modern wooden fishing plug had its beginnings around 1900, and in the following years several companies started to manufacture these lures for black bass. Later they made larger and stronger plugs for pike, muskellunge, and salmon.

Plugs are now widely used in freshwater fishing, as a look at any fishing tackle store showcase or counter will reveal. Today there are many different types, sizes, shapes, and colors or finishes of plugs on the market. The angler who wants to make his own plugs can duplicate many of the more popular models. However, there are a few basic types, and the construction of these will be covered in this chapter.

To make plugs you will need wood that can be cut into small blocks and then shaped to the size and form you require. The best all-around wood for making fishing plugs is cedar. Straight-grained white cedar is excellent since it is light, strong, and easy to work. It also stands up better in the water than most woods. Red cedar can also be used instead of the white variety. Other woods that can be used for making plugs are basswood and birch.

Most of the woods mentioned above can be obtained at a lumber yard in large blocks or round logs. They can then be sawed with a circular saw or hand saw into convenient small blocks about 6 inches long and about 1½ inches square.

The fastest way to shape wooden plugs is with a lathe. With a wood-turning lathe, or even a small metal-turning lathe for that matter, you can shape the plugs quickly and uniformly in fairly large numbers. If you already have such a lathe, so much the better.

When turning down plugs with a lathe, mount one of the wooden blocks between the centers. Measure and mark the length of the plug you are making on the wooden block with a pencil so that you know where both ends will fall. Then start the lathe and, using the wood-turning tools, shape the wood to the correct diameter, taper, and shape of the model you are copying. After this is done, take some sandpaper and sand the plug very smooth as it is turning. Then cut the finished plug off from the rest of the wood.

If you have no lathe you can turn out plugs at a fair speed with ordinary hand tools. You can whittle plugs from the softer woods with an ordinary sharp knife if you prefer to work that way. However, a somewhat easier and quicker method is to secure the block of wood in a bench vise and then use a rasp to take off the corners. If you cut the block of wood almost the diameter of the finished plug, you will have less filing to do. In other words, if the finished plug will be an inch in diameter, start with a block of wood of about the same diameter or a bit more. Then you only have to round off the corners with a rasp. After using the rasp for the rough work, finish shaping the plug with a wood file. Then it can be made smooth by using different grades of sandpaper.

Several basic body shapes are used in making freshwater plugs. An old-time favorite is the "wobbler" type shown in Fig. 1. This plug is simple to make since it is uniform in thickness with a rounded tail and a grooved head. It should be about 3¾ inches long and ¾ inch in diameter. The dimensions given for all the wooden plugs here are the so-called bait-casting size. These are fairly large freshwater plugs suitable for use with bait-casting, spin-casting, or spinning rods. They weigh about ½ to ⅝ of an ounce when finished. If you want

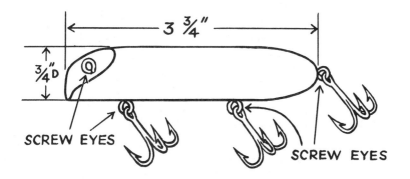

Wobbler plug.   *Figure 1.*

smaller plugs strictly for use with light spinning tackle, make them about one-third smaller than the dimensions given here.

A simple way to make the wobbler-type plug is to cut the head at a forty-five-degree angle, as shown in Fig. 2. However, most of these plugs are made with a grooved head. To do this, cut the plug at the same angle, then carve out the head with a rotary file mounted in a drill press or hand motor tool. If you haven't got such power tools, use a small gouge to cut out the groove in the head of the plug.

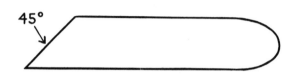

Figure 2.   *Simple wobbler plug with 45° angle head.*

To complete the wobbler plug you'll need three treble hooks and four screw eyes. To start the screw eye in the wood, first take an ice pick or awl and push it into the wood where the screw eyes will go to make small starting holes. Then put the screw eyes into the holes and twist them in. The screw eye that goes at the head of the plug (where the fishing line is tied) is forced in as is. Pliers can be used to screw it in. The other three screw eyes hold hooks, and if the screw eyes are closed they must be opened. Then slip on a treble hook over the eye and close it with pliers. If you want to give the plug a professional look, slip small disk or cup washers over the shank of the screw eye before you force it into the plug body (see Fig. 3). Two treble hooks are attached below the plug and the third at the rear or tail.

Screw eyes make inexpensive, simple hook hangers and are strong enough for most freshwater fish. However, you can also use special hook hangers to attach the treble hooks. These are small, metal saddles with a stop that prevents the hook from fouling with other hooks or the fishing line on a cast, or when the lure strikes the water. The hook hangers have two small holes on each end and are attached to the plug with small screws, as shown in Fig. 4.

Next we have the surface plugs, which ride on top of the water and create some kind of commotion, such as a splash or ripple. One of the simplest of these is the "popper" type. It is easy to make a popping plug, using the same plug body as the wobbler plug de-

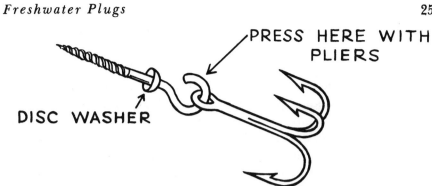

Figure 3.   *Treble hook on screw eye.*

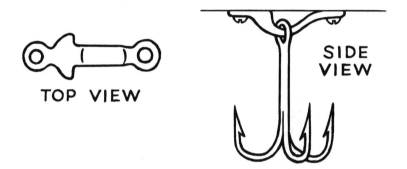

Figure 4.   *Hook hanger.*

scribed above. You simply turn the plug around and attach the hooks on the opposite side, as shown in Fig. 5. Here you do not necessarily

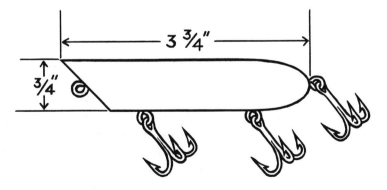

Popping plug with three treble hooks.   *Figure 5.*

need a grooved head. A head cut at a forty-five-degree angle will provide plenty of splash and commotion when jerked. This plug is also made with three treble hooks. However, if you are making a smaller version of this plug for use with spinning tackle, it can have only two treble hooks—one at the belly and the other at the tail.

The typical popping type of surface plug is shown in Fig. 6. This plug has a wide, cupped head and then tapers to a narrow tail. It should be about 2¾ inches long with the head section 1⅛ inches in diameter and tapering to a tail about ⅜ inch thick. This lure has one screw eye at the head in the center of the cupped head for the line and two treble hooks, one at the belly and the other at the tail. Because of its shape, this popping plug is most easily made when turned down on a lathe. However, if you don't mind the work involved, you can whittle or file it down to shape with hand tools.

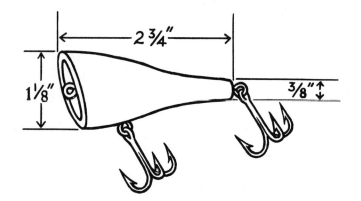

Another typical popping plug.   *Figure 6.*

Another type of surface plug that was popular many years ago and is still a good fish getter is the "collar" type shown in Fig. 7. It is easily turned down on a lathe in a short time. Make it about 3 inches long and ¾ inch in diameter, the collar extending about ¼ inch from the rest of the body. Since this collar encircles the plug it makes a foolproof splasher, no matter how it lands in the water. When jerked it will throw a spray that attracts fish. This plug has one screw eye at the head or nose and two treble hooks, one at the belly and the other at the tail.

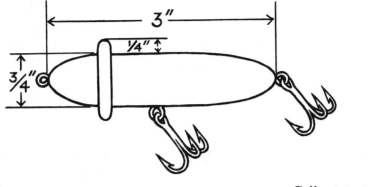

Figure 7.   *Collar type plug.*

Another surface plug that has proven effective over the years is the "propeller" type (Fig. 8). This plug has one or two propellers, usually one at the head and another at the tail. When it is retrieved or jerked the propeller blades revolve and throw a spray. Although

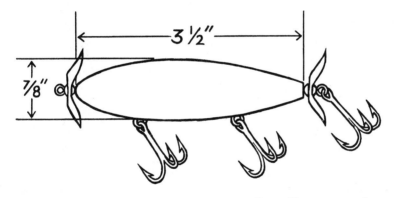

Figure 8.   *Propeller type surface plug.*

screw eyes can be used to hold the propeller blades, a much better and stronger method is to rig this plug with a wire running through the center as shown in Fig. 9. When making this plug, drill a hole through the center, from the head to the tail. If you have a drill press, do this with an extra long drill and a jig, which will hold the plug body in the correct position. You can also drill such a hole very easily with a long hand drill—if you do it before the plug is

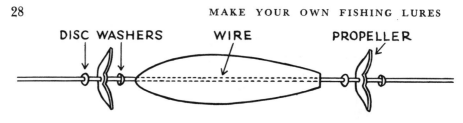

Figure 9.   *Assembly of propeller plug.*

shaped. In other words, drill the hole in the rectangular block of wood through the center, then rasp or file to finish it off. Then find the center of the block of wood and draw an X from corner to corner.

The propellers for this plug can be cut out of thin sheet brass as shown in Fig. 10. You can do some cutting with hand snips, then use flat and triangular files to finish the job. A hole must then be drilled in the propeller. Finally, twist the blades in opposite directions and slant them back so that they will spin.

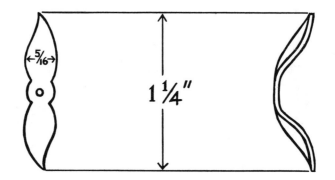

Shape and size of propeller.   *Figure 10.*

To assemble this plug you need some wire such as the hardened brass or steel wire. Cut a short length, allowing enough on both ends of the plug for eyes, then using the round-nosed pliers, form an eye on one end (instructions for doing this can be found in chap 14). But before you complete the eye, slip on a treble hook. Then slip on a tiny washer, which will act as a bearing for the propeller blade. This can be a disk or cup washer, a grommet, or even a bead, whichever is available. Next, slip on the propeller blade, add another washer, and run the wire through the wood plug body from the rear or tail. Slip on another washer, then the second propeller blade, and finally the last washer. Now form the second eye in front to which the line will be attached. To complete the plug screw in another treble hook at the belly.

Another effective plug is the "darter" type shown in Fig. 11. This plug is 3¾ inches long with a head about ¾ inch in diameter and tapering to a tail of ⅜ inch thick. The head slopes downward, starting about one inch from the end. Then a small notch is cut or filed at the nose of the plug. This plug also has three treble hooks attached, two at the belly and one at the tail. The screw eye for holding the fishing line is screwed in at the top of the head where it slopes.

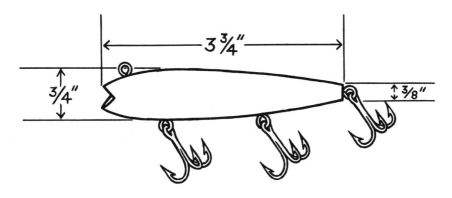

Darter type plug.   *Figure 11.*

The strictly "underwater" plug shown in Fig. 12 is an old-time favorite that has taken freshwater fish consistently through the years. The large bait-casting sizes in this plug consists of a body about 4 inches long and ¾ inch in diameter, and the tail tapers to ⅜ of an inch. The head part is round with a concave cut on top. This can easily be done with a half-round file or by holding the plug against a revolving grindstone.

The underwater plug requires a metal lip that makes it dive, wriggle, and travel under the water. The shape and dimensions of

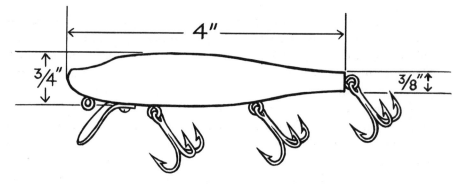

Figure 12.   *Underwater plug.*

this lip are shown in Fig. 13. It can be cut out from sheet brass and
two holes are drilled to take small screws for fastening the lip to the
wood body. Although a straight metal lip will give the plug some
action, better results are obtained if the lip is bent like a shallow plate or saucer. This can be done by hammering the metal lip
gently with a small ball peen hammer. The hammering can be done
against a block of hard wood that has a depression gouged out to
take the metal lip.

When assembling the underwater plug start by screwing in a
screw eye under the head to which the line will be attached. Then
fasten on the metal lip with two small screws just behind this screw

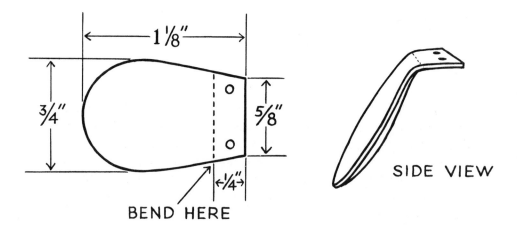

Figure 13.   *Metal lip for underwater plug.*

eye. Next, about an inch behind the metal lip, screw in one of the treble hooks. A second treble hook is attached about midway between the first one and the tail, and the final treble hook is attached to the tail.

The "jointed" plug is easily made by using the same body as the underwater plug described above, only here you cut the wood body in half, as shown in Fig. 14. The two parts are then connected by screw eyes. The rest of the plug is assembled in much the same way as the one-piece underwater plug, except that only two instead of three treble hooks are used.

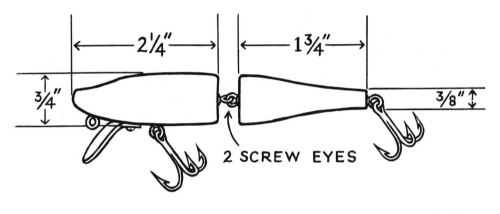

Jointed underwater plug. *Figure 14.*

As mentioned before, the dimensions given here are for the larger bait-casting sizes. These plugs will run from about ½ to ¾ ounces in weight. But you don't have to follow the dimensions given here—make the plugs smaller or larger if you want to! The small spinning size plugs can be made one-third smaller and these will weigh between ¼ and ½ ounce. The bait-casting sizes described above are ideal for bass, pike, muskies, coho salmon, and lake trout. You can make still bigger ones for muskies and lake trout.

The treble hooks used on the larger bait-casting-size plugs should be either sizes No. 1 or 1/0. For the smaller spinning size, No. 2 or 4 are more suitable. Such hooks can be bought in most fishing-tackle stores or you can order them from some of the mail-order houses listed in the back of this book.

If you haven't got the time or desire to turn out the plug bodies with hand tools, you can also order different types and sizes of finished wood bodies from some of these mail-order houses. These wooden bodies are already shaped and sanded smooth so that all you have to do is assemble the parts, such as hardware and hooks. If you want to make plastic plugs, order such bodies from the mail-order houses. Some of these plastic plug bodies come complete, all ready for adding the hooks and other metal parts. Others come in two sections and must be cemented together.

Before making the wooden plugs described above, decide how they will be painted. If you plan to dip the plug bodies in enamel or lacquer or spray them with an airbrush or can, this should be done before they are assembled. If you plan to paint them with a small brush, assemble the plugs first and paint them later on.

If several wood bodies are to be painted at the same time, you'll find the quickest method is to dip them into a can of white lacquer or enamel. Before you do this, screw in a small screw eye or a hook into the tail for holding while dipping and hanging for drying (see Fig. 15). For best results, the lacquer or enamel should be fairly thin, and after the plug body is dipped once it should be allowed to dry, then dipped again as many times as it is necessary to get a good, thick coat. Usually this base coat will take three or four dippings.

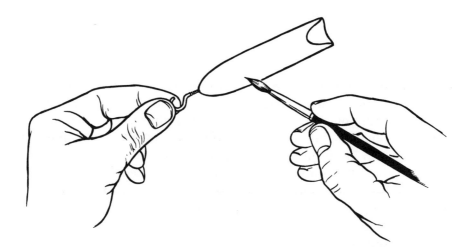

Figure 15.   Screw eye or hook for holding plug body while it is being painted, sprayed, or dipped.

You can also spray on solid colors such as white or silver with an airbrush, or by using one of those pressurized paint cans that can be bought in any hardware or paint store. These cans are handy to use and the colors dry fast.

If you paint the wood bodies by hand with a brush, you'll find enamel easiest to handle. It can be applied fairly thick and usually two coats of white will do the job.

After you have applied the white base coat and it is dry, you are ready to apply other colors. A simple way to make a red-and-white plug is to use a strip of masking tape all around the plug about an inch from the nose (see Fig. 16). Then spray or paint the head part with bright red. When it dries you can remove the masking tape and you'll have a clean, sharp dividing line between the red and white.

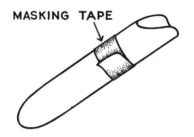

Tape around a plug, when painting or spraying a red head.   Figure 16.

Another good color combination for freshwater plugs is a lure with a light blue or green back and silver sides. This looks like many of the minnows found in freshwater lakes and rivers. To apply these colors start with an all-white plug and brush on light blue or green enamel. When the color is still wet, brush on silver or aluminum paint along both sides of the plug. Where the silver meets the light blue or green, blend colors until they are well mixed.

To make a natural scale finish on a wood plug, spray blue, green, or brown over the top or back and sides of the basic white-bodied plug. Leave the belly of the plug white. When this dries use a cloth netting tacked loosely on a wooden frame to apply the scale finish. Hold the plug against this netting from the opposite side while you spray on the silver with a can or an artist's airbrush. To get a real professional finish on your plugs you need an artist's airbrush such

Artist airbrush.   *Figure 17.*

as the Paasche type (Fig. 17). With the airbrush you'll need a tank
of compressed air or a compressor motor. The artist's type airbrush
results in fine work and you get the best results with it when making
scale finishes or other patterns. With such an airbrush, also, you can
work out various color combinations, blends, and soft edges that will
give them a real professional look. But if you have no airbrush, don't
despair—with a little practice you can do a pretty good paint job
with a brush.

After the plugs are painted you may want to give them a more
complete look by adding eyes, although eyes are not necessary to
catch fish. Most store-bought plugs have glass eyes. These are similar to the eyes used by taxidermists and can be obtained from them.
They are mounted on wire that is clipped off with cutting pliers, leaving a short length of wire about ¼ inch long. Then drill holes in the
plug, put in some quick-drying cement, and insert the glass eyes into
the shallow holes. You can also paint the eyes with a small, pointed
brush or dab them on with a flat head nail dipped in yellow paint.
After the yellow dries use a small flat head nail dipped in black to
apply the pupil of the eye (see Fig. 18).

The fishing plugs described above and the suggestions for making
them are just a starter for the ingenious or ambitious "do-it-yourself"
angler. Many different kinds of plugs can be made or you can create
or design your own. The angler can experiment with plug weights,
sizes, and shapes and work out a lure most suitable for the waters
he fishes. One angler may want big, strong plugs to use for such large
fish as muskies, pike, salmon, and lake trout. Naturally he will use
larger plug bodies, stronger, heavier hooks, and heavy hardware and

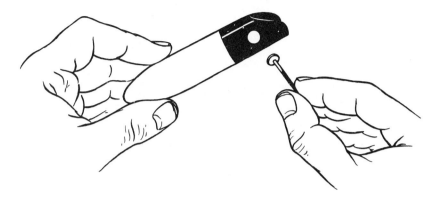

Figure 18. *Using a flat-head nail to paint eyes on a plug.*

fittings. Another angler may want small, light lures to use for such small fish as trout, bass, and panfish. He will make much smaller plugs and use lighter hooks and hardware. Still another angler may want to create a plug that resembles some particular minnow or small fish or animal that fish feed on in the waters he fishes.

All of these anglers can usually meet such demands more quickly by making or designing their own fishing plugs.

3

FRESHWATER SPIN BUGS

One of the most effective lures for black bass in fresh water is the so-called bass bug, which is used with a fly rod. However, these bugs are too light to cast with a casting or spinning rod. But the angler who wants to use such tackle can easily make bass bugs that are heavy enough to cast.

Such lures (which I will call *spin bugs* to separate them from the regular cork or plastic *bass bugs*) should weigh at least ¼ ounce or a bit more to cast well. They are usually bulky, having hair or feathers that hold them back during the cast.

Spin bugs or bass bugs are usually made to resemble some kind of insect or bug that has fallen into the water. These are generally such big insects as dragonflies, butterflies, moths, beetles, grasshoppers, and caterpillars. Such insects usually float and kick around on top of the water, so spin bugs that do the same are the best fish-getters. However, some of these lures are also made to resemble minnows, small fish, or frogs.

The simplest type of spin bug one can make is a small popping bug much along the same lines as the popping plugs covered in the previous chapter. However, the spin bugs are much smaller, shorter, and have fewer hooks. And they will have hair or feathers added to imitate the legs or wings of a bug or insect.

The popping spin bug illustrated in Fig. 19 can be made from soft, light wood such as cedar or basswood. It should be about 1½ inches long and ⅞ inch in diameter. The head slants downward at the regular forty-five-degree angle. You need two small screw eyes and one treble hook to finish this bug. One screw eye goes at the head for the fishing line, while the other one holds the treble hook at the tail. The screw eyes and hooks should be smaller than those used for the regular freshwater plugs covered in chapter 2. A No. 2 or No. 4 treble hook is a good size to use. The hooks should be sharp, fine-wire types of the best quality. You'll hook more fish with needle-sharp hooks than with dull, cheap ones.

Before the treble hook is put on, the screw eye should be wound with bucktail hair, as shown in Fig. 20. First cut your bucktail hair so that it is only slightly longer than the shank of the hook. Next, get some fly-tying thread and make a few turns with it around the hook shank near the eye. Now form three or four pinches of the bucktail hair and have them ready. Take one of the pinches of bucktail, lay it against the hook shank and wind several turns of thread around it. Add another pinch of bucktail next to the first one and wind some thread around it. Keep doing this until the hook shank is completely covered by the bucktail. Finish off the wrapping with more turns and bind it with a whip finish or a series of half hitches. Then coat the thread wrapping with fly-tying cement or with one of the clear lacquers or cements that come in tubes. Clear nail polish can also be used.

To make the wings of the spin bug that project from the sides, use bucktail or other hair. Take two pinches of the bucktail and wrap the butts tightly with fly-tying thread, as shown in Fig. 21. Then dip or dab the windings with the clear, waterproof cement or lacquer. After they dry, drill two holes in the wood body of the bug, one on each side. When you do this, make sure the holes are just big enough to take the butts or ends of the bucktail wings snugly. In other words, it should be a tight fit. Then dip the butts of the wings in clear cement and insert them into the holes. You can also force a drop or two of the cement into the holes with a stick or small brush. When the cement dries, the bucktail wings will be held firmly in place.

Another type of popping spin bug can be made using the plug body of the popping plug described in the previous chapter. Only here you cut off the tail section so that the bug is short, as shown in Fig. 22. These bugs can also have a treble hook wound with bucktail hair and wings at the sides like the bug described before this one.

A third kind of popping spin bug is shown in Fig. 23. For this one you use the same size wooden body as the popping bug shown in Fig. 19. However, instead of attaching a free-swinging treble hook you add a single hook to the underside of the body. A regular shank hook about size No. 2/0 can be used. To attach this hook, first drill a shallow hole underneath the body, about half an inch from the tail end. This hole should be round enough and deep enough to take the

Figure 19.

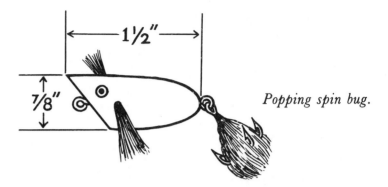

Popping spin bug.

Figure 20.

Tail hook wound with
bucktail.

Figure 21.

Winding bucktail hair to
make wings.

Figure 22.

Using the front part of
a plug body to make a
spin bug.

SIDE VIEW   TOP VIEW

Popping spin bug with a single hook.   *Figure 23.*

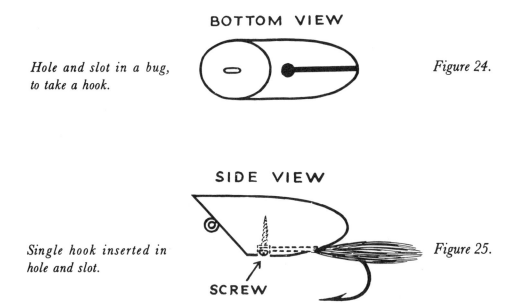

BOTTOM VIEW

Hole and slot in a bug,   *Figure 24.*
to take a hook.

SIDE VIEW

Single hook inserted in   *Figure 25.*
hole and slot.

SCREW

round eye of the hook. The next step is to slit a narrow groove in the wood, running from the hole to the end of the body. This will accommodate the hook shank (see Fig. 24). Now wind some bucktail on the hook shank, about a half inch from the eye of the hook, then force the hook eye and shank into the hole and slot. After this get a small screw eye and screw it through the hook eye. This will hold the hook firmly in place (see Fig. 25). Then get some plastic wood and fill up the hole and slit to conform to the round body shape of the bug. To complete the bug wrap on two feather wings on the top or sides of the body. The tying thread can be wound completely around the body to hold the feathers in place. Then dab some clear cement on the winding and paint over this winding when the cement dries to hide the winding.

Such single-hook spin bugs can easily be made weedless by adding a wire hook guard made from fine stainless steel wire or piano wire. Use a nail or thick wire to help form the eye of the guard, and it should look like Fig. 26 and be long enough to extend beyond the point of the hook when in place. When making the single-hook spin bug with a weed guard, this wire is slipped on the small screw first, then the hook. In other words, the same screw holds both the wire guard and the hook in place.

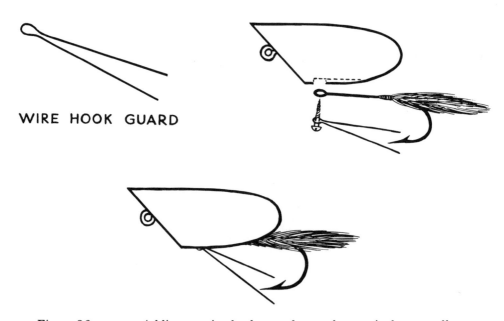

WIRE HOOK GUARD

Figure 26.   Adding a wire hook guard to make a spin bug weedless.

The next spin bug is the silent type, which has a pointed nose instead of a cupped or slanted head. This type of bug resembles a minnow or some other kind of small fish more than it does a bug or insect. It swims through the water creating a ripple like a minnow cleaving the surface of a river or lake. The construction and dimensions of this lure are shown in Fig. 27. The wood body should be about 1½ inches long and ¾ inch in diameter. The quick way to make this bug is to fasten a screw eye in the nose and another one

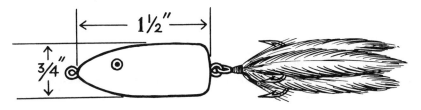

Silent type spin bug.   *Figure 27.*

at the tail, for a free-swinging treble hook or a single hook. The treble will tend to hook more fish on a surface strike, but the single hook will snag less in the weeds. To give this bug a minnow appearance the hook should be wrapped with four to six rooster hackle feathers, long enough and wide enough to cover the treble (or single) hook. When tying these feathers on the hook, wrap a few turns of the thread under them to make them splay out. In other words, try to make the hackles slant out away from the hook. This will give them a "breathing" action in the water. If you want to, tie in another hackle feather near the hook eye, then wind it around the hook to form a collar of hackle.

To make a stronger bug of this type, run a wire through the wood body from nose to tail and form eyes at each end to take the line and the hook. And, instead of using hackle feathers, tie some long bucktail around the hook shank.

A somewhat heavier and larger type of spin bug can be made as shown in Fig. 28. This is also a minnow type of lure since it is shaped more like a small fish than an insect. However, if you want to do so, it can be dressed up with wings or other hair or feathers

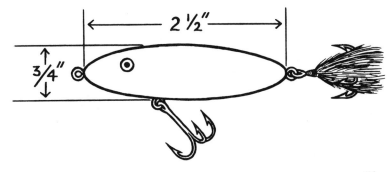

Minnow type spin bug.   *Figure 28.*

on the body to resemble a very large bug. The way it stands with a streamlined body and only a few feathers on the hook makes it an excellent casting lure when used with a spinning outfit. The body can be about 2½ inches long and ¾ inch in diameter at the thickest part in the center. It tapers to a rounded nose and tail on both ends. Small screw eyes can be used at the nose, under the belly, and at the tail to hold the two treble hooks. The rear treble hook can be wound with short bucktail hair.

Spin bugs can also be made to imitate small frogs, which are a favorite food of black bass, pickerel, and pike. You can easily make such a bug as shown in Fig. 29. The wood body should be 1¾ inches long and about ⅞ inch wide. In depth it can be about ⅝ inch thick. The head is cut out as shown in the side-view drawing in Fig. 29. To make this lure you need a regular-length shank hook with a hump such as those used for tying cork bass bugs. First wrap the hook shank with fine fly-tying thread and then cut a slot in the belly of the wood body to accommodate the hook. Make sure that you cut a groove deep enough to take the hump of the hook. The next step is to put some clear, quick-drying cement both on the wrapped hook shank and inside the slot of the wood body. You can use a thin knife blade to force this cement into the slot. Then push the hook shank into the slot of the wood body and fix it in a permanent position. When the cement dries, fill the slot with plastic wood. To finish off this bug, drill holes near the head to add a couple of short pinches of bucktail hair to simulate legs and then drill two more holes near the tail and insert two longer pinches of bucktail to imitate the long rear legs of a frog.

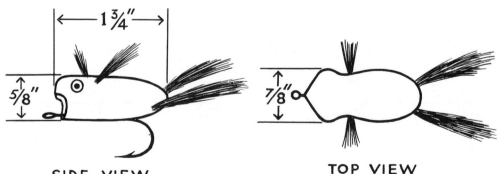

SIDE VIEW   TOP VIEW

Figure 29.   *Frog type spin bug.*

The spin bugs described above are made from wood and have enough weight to cast with a light spinning outfit. You can also make them from cork, but you'll have to add some lead to provide enough weight for casting. For this you'll need some sheet lead and lead wire. If you have trouble getting sheet lead you can always get some lead sinkers or weights and pound them flat with a hammer. Lead wire can be obtained from some of the mail-order supply houses.

Before I go into the methods of loading a cork bug with lead I will describe the basic construction of such a bug. You can obtain cork cylinders or cork bass bug bodies, already shaped and sanded smooth, from the mail-order houses and fly-tying suppliers (see back of this book). These cork bodies come in various lengths and thicknesses, but for best results use the largest sizes.

To make a cork bug you'll need some long-shank double-hump hooks as shown in Fig. 30. Sizes No. 1/0 and 2/0 are best for spin bugs. The hook shank is then wrapped with fine fly-tying thread along the shank, which will be buried in the cork body. This wrapping provides a better gripping and holding surface than the smooth metal of the bare hook.

Figure 30.   *Long shank double-hump hook.*

The next step is to cut a slot along the bottom of the cork lengthwise, to take the hook. This can be done with a single-edge razor blade or you can use a small saw such as a hacksaw. This slot should be just deep enough to bury the hook shank in the body (see Fig. 31). Another method often used is to cut out a triangular wedge along the bottom as shown in Fig. 31. Whichever method you use, coat the wrapped hook shank with clear, waterproof cement and, if you have a slot in your cork body, also force some cement into it. Some anglers prefer to use a waterproof marine glue such as the plastic resin type instead of the clear cement. Both are good, although the plastic resin glue is somewhat stronger and more permanent.

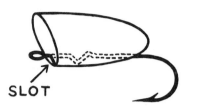

SLOT

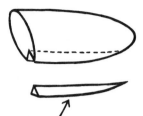

SECTION CUT FROM BODY

Figure 31.   *Cork bug bodies prepared for the hook.*

After the hook shank has been covered with cement and you have worked some of the cement into the cork body, force the hook into the slot. Then wrap the cork body fairly tightly with some cord to press the slot together while the cement dries.

If you cut a triangular wedge out of your cork body, coat your hook shank with cement or glue and push it in place into the cork body. Then add more cement or glue to the spot that has been cut out and also to the wedge itself. Put the triangular wedge back in place and tie some cord around the cork body to hold it in place while drying.

To add lead weight to a cork spin bug, use a cork body shaped like a bottle stopper. In other words don't round off the tail part, but leave it flat like a cork bottle stopper. Then cut a round piece from a sheet of lead to fit neatly at the tail end of the cork body. If you are using a single hook on your spin bug, cut a small slot in the lead so that the weight can be slipped over the hook. Then drill a hole in the center of the round lead weight to accommodate a small screw. Now coat both the tail end of the cork body and the lead weight with cement and screw the lead piece in place on the cork (see Fig. 32).

If you are making a spin bug with a treble hook instead of a single hook, you go through the same steps. Of course, you do not need a slot in the lead weight now—only a small hole in the center of the round lead. You can slip this lead onto the wire used in the "through-the-body" construction of this type of spin bug, then form a wire eye at the tail to take the hook. You can also cement or glue the lead weight onto the cork body, but the wire eye will keep it in position if formed tightly against the lead.

When making a spin bug with a pointed or rounded tail, wait until the lure is finished with feathers or hair. Then get some of the

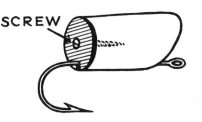

SCREW

LEAD WEIGHT WITH
HOLE AND SLOT

WEIGHT IN PLACE
ON CORK BODY

Figure 32.   *Adding a lead weight to a cork bug.*

lead wire and wind it around the hook shank next to the cork body or wind the lead wire around the cork body itself (see Fig. 33). In any of these operations, always make sure you do not add too much lead weight, otherwise the cork body will sit too low in the water or will be cocked at the wrong angle or even sink.

To finish off the cork spin bugs add hackle feathers at the tail and wings on the body as described for the wood-type spin bugs earlier.

LEAD
WIRE

LEAD WIRE

Figure 33.   *Cork bugs weighted with lead wire.*

In painting any of the wood- or cork-body spin bugs use enamels or lacquers. If you want to, dip the body three or four times in the color before you add the hair or feathers. Or if you have an airbrush or spray can you can spray the bugs any color you want. A quick and easy way to paint them with a brush is to use the fast-drying "dope" used by model airplane builders. This comes in many colors and you can add one coat after another in a short time. Wood will require only two or three coats, but cork is more porous and rougher and may take more coats.

You can use any color combinations you want on the spin bugs, but the most effective ones are usually black body and wings, brown body and wings, or yellow body and wings. A bug with a white body and white tail or wings is easily seen and is as effective as most colors. When making the silent minnow-type bug, use silver or gold paint on the sides of the body or a scale finish. The frog-type bug can have a white or yellow belly and green back with spots.

You can also give spin bugs a fuzzy or hair finish on the body. This is done by first painting the bug the color you want, then giving it a coat of clear cement or celluloid enamel. Then while it is still wet, sprinkle with bits of hair, wool, or floss. These materials, of course, have to be prepared in advance by cutting or chopping up the hair, wool, or fur.

Still another finish on spin bugs can be obtained by using flitters. These are small metallic chips of gold or silver that can be scattered on the wet coat of cement or clear celluloid enamel of the bug body. They are given a coat of clear lacquer afterward to prevent the metallic chips from tarnishing.

Although many bugs made professionally have glass eyes, these are not really necessary. It is much quicker and less expensive to paint on the eyes or dab them on as described and shown in chapter 2. You can also obtain decal eyes from some of the fly-tying and mail-order houses and paste these on quickly.

4

SALTWATER PLUGS

There are many reasons why you should make your own saltwater fishing plugs. First, of course, is to save some money, since the larger plugs are quite expensive if bought in a store. Anglers also lose more saltwater plugs than freshwater plugs. It is possible to fish with one plug in fresh water for many years. But you're lucky if you don't lose some saltwater plugs after a few days of fishing. The fishing line may break on a cast, or the plug may get tangled around piles, rocks, or weeds. Or you may cut your line on barnacles, mussels, or coral. Also, big saltwater fish are tough fighters and are always breaking lines and taking the plugs with them. Finally, the wear and tear on saltwater plugs quickly ruins the paint and the wood body and rusts the hooks. A saltwater fisherman has to keep on replacing lost or ruined plugs.

Furthermore, fishing with saltwater plugs is comparatively new. Fishing with such plugs didn't really become popular in salt water until after World War II, so there is still plenty of room for creating and experimenting with such lures. Many saltwater anglers enjoy creating new plugs or trying to improve the old ones. They add stronger hooks, rearrange hooks, make plugs of different shapes, sizes, and weights, and try out different color schemes.

Saltwater plugs can also be made from cedar, and this is the best wood to use for the smaller-type plugs. This light wood has the buoyancy to support metal parts such as lips, screw eyes, screws, and hooks without sinking. The use of cedar is especially important when making surface plugs. But cedar may be too light for the larger-sized saltwater plugs, unless weighted with lead. Hence, many surf anglers who use big plugs make them from heavier woods such as birch, fir, maple, and walnut. Even such hard woods as ash, oak, and hickory have been used successfully when a heavy saltwater plug is required. However these woods are tough to cut, drill, or shape with hand tools and they do not support too many hardware parts without sinking. In fact, when making any saltwater surface plugs it is necessary to check carefully to make certain that the wood body will support the metal plates, screw eyes, screws, hooks, and other hardware without sinking. All surface plugs should float for best results.

I find that it's a good idea to assemble all the metal parts that will go on a certain plug and strap them on the wood body with a rubber band or Scotch tape. Then place the wooden plug body in a pail or bathtub filled with water. If it doesn't sink or submerge too much you are safe in using all that metal on the plug. Otherwise you have to make a larger wooden body or use lighter hardware such as screws, screw eyes, metal plates, or hooks.

In saltwater fishing the deadliest type of plug is usually a surface model. The easiest plug of this type to make is the simple popper shown in Fig. 34. This plug can be about 6½ inches long and have

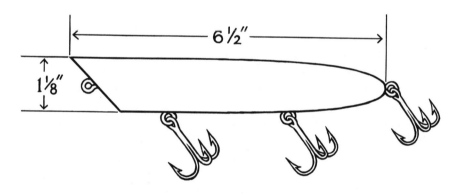

Simple type of salt-water popper plug.   *Figure 34.*

a diameter of 1⅛ inches. The head can be straight cut at a forty-five-degree angle. The plug is equipped with three 5/0 extra-strong hooks. The quickest way to attach these hooks to the body is by means of screw eyes, which should be fairly large and of heavy wire and long, deep threads. The best screw eyes are made of brass, since they don't rust in salt water. However, you can also use galvanized iron screws if they are heavy and strong. If this popper is made from a heavy wood it will cast far without additional weight. But if you use light wood or want as heavy a plug as possible, add some lead to the tail end of the plug as shown in Fig. 35. You drill a hole and plug it up with a round chunk of lead. If you make a tight fit you can tap in the lead after putting some cement in the hole.

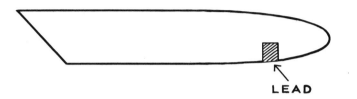

LEAD

Position of lead weight in plug body.   *Figure   35.*

Heavy screws will usually prove satisfactory as hook holders and for attaching the line to the plugs described here. For stronger plugs, however, attach the hooks by using hook hangers similar to the one used for freshwater plugs. For saltwater plugs, such a hook hanger must be heavier than that used for freshwater plugs. You can make such hook hangers by using a brass piece $1\frac{1}{2}$ inches long by $\frac{1}{4}$ inch wide and $\frac{1}{32}$ inch thick. File the brass in a bench vise as shown in Fig. 36. Then bend it with round-nosed and flat-nosed pliers so that the finished hook hanger will look like the one shown in the illustration.

To make the saltwater plugs still stronger, use the "through-wire" construction method shown in Fig. 37. Here you drill a hole through the center of the plug body from the nose to the tail. Then drill larger-diameter holes in the belly of the plug to meet the small-

STOCK   FILE LIKE THIS   BEND LIKE THIS

Figure 36.   *Making a hook hanger from brass stock.*

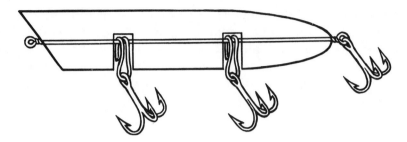

Figure 37.   *Through-wire construction and wire hook hangers.*

er hole through the middle of the body. Next, make some hook hangers from brass or stainless-steel wire (see the illustration of such a hook hanger in Fig. 38). Then get about a ten- or twelve-inch length of brass or steel wire, form an eye on one end, and insert the other end of the wire in the nose of the plug. Attach a treble hook to one of the hook hangers and insert this into the hole at the belly of the plug. At the same time, push the wire rod through the plug to catch this hook hanger through the double loop. You can easily test to see that the hanger is caught on the wire by pulling on the treble hook. After the first treble hook is caught, insert the second hanger and

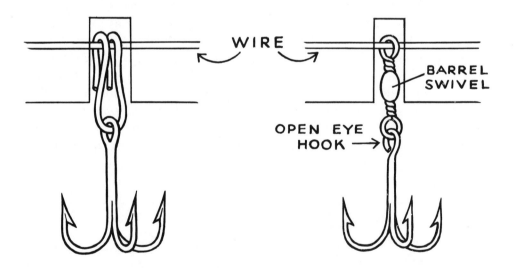

Figure 38.   *Two types of hook hangers used with through-wire construction plugs.*

hook and catch that with the wire and then push the wire out through the rear of the plug. To finish it, form an eye at the tail, but before closing the eye slide on another treble hook.

Instead of making a wire hook hanger, you can use barrel swivels for hook hangers as shown in Fig. 38. They have two eyes: the eye inside the body of the plug is caught by the wire and the eye outside the plug holds the hook. To attach the hooks you must either obtain treble hooks that can be opened at the eye or cut the eye with a hacksaw so that it can be spread to take the hook and then clamped shut. You can also attach the hook to the barrel swivel eye by first forcing on a split ring, then attaching the hook to the ring. If you use brass split rings you can solder them so that they can't open.

Another strong way to attach a treble hook to a wooden plug is to drill holes in the belly and tail of the plug to take hook hangers such as barrel swivels. Then drill smaller diameter holes from one side of the plug body to the other. Care must be taken here to meet the larger hole of the barrel swivel. Then insert the hook hanger or barrel swivel with the treble hook into the big hole. Finally, drive a brass or copper pin or nail through the small hole to catch the hook hanger or barrel swivel eye.

Another large popper that you can make is shown in Fig. 39. This has a tapered body about 7 inches long and a diameter of 1¼ inches at the head. The head is cupped or gouged out to create a commotion and splash in the water when the plug is jerked. This plug can have three 5/0 or 6/0 treble hooks, two at the belly and one at the tail. They can be attached by any of the methods described above. The plug, if made of light wood, can be loaded at the belly or tail with lead, if you want.

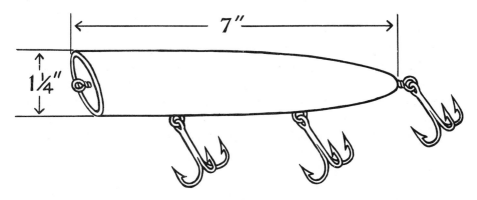

Popper with cupped head.   *Figure 39.*

A somewhat smaller popper is the bomber type shown in Fig. 40. This is narrow at the head and thicker in diameter at the tail. Because of this shape, it casts like a bullet even into a stiff wind. The plug shown here is heavy enough to use with a conventional surf rod or with a surf spinning rod. It measures about 5 inches long and has a diameter of 1¼ inches at the tail and ⅞ inch at the head. The head is cut at a slant of forty-five-degrees. Two 5/0 treble hooks are attached, one at the belly near the head and the other at the tail.

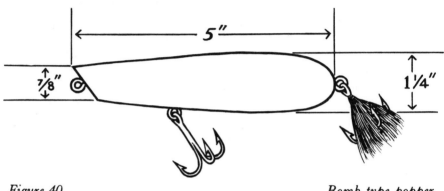

Figure 40.   *Bomb type popper.*

The large surface plugs described above are used mostly for surf fishing or casting from a boat for big fish with fairly heavy tackle. If you want to make up smaller saltwater surface plugs to use with light spinning or casting tackle, just make a smaller version of any of the models above. For example, if you want to make a small surface popper of the type shown in Fig. 41, make the same way as the large one (Fig. 39) but smaller and lighter. It could have a body 4 inches long with a diameter of ⅞ inch. Instead of using three treble hooks, you need only two and these can be smaller such as size No. 1/0 or 2/0. But make sure they are made of heavy wire instead of thin wire.

Another effective surface popper can be made by using the same size plug body as the freshwater wobbler shown in Fig. 1. However, instead of using it as shown there, turn the body around and use it as in Fig. 42. Now, instead of diving or wobbling, it becomes a small surface popper that throws a big splash when jerked. It also can use two treble hooks in sizes No. 1/0 or 2/0.

You can use the surface popper plugs above as they are, or you can tie some white or yellow bucktail hair around the treble hook at

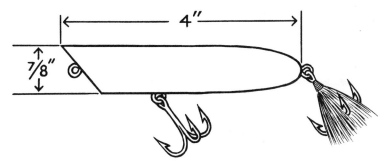

Figure 41.   *Small salt-water popper.*

Popper made from wobbler type body.   *Figure 42.*

the tail. Do not put on too much hair, especially on the smaller and lighter plugs, or you won't get as much distance on the cast.

Other surface saltwater plugs include the swimming type shown in Fig. 43. This plug can have a body about 6½ inches long and a diameter of 1¼ inches at the head. It tapers at the tail to about ⅝ inch. This plug has a metal lip of the type and size shown in Fig. 44, which can be cut from sheet brass or stainless steel. If you use stainless steel, you can use a lighter gauge than if you use brass because it has more spring and is tougher to cut and work if it is thick. The metal lip is bent and a hole is drilled as shown. For this plug the through-wire construction is most practical to hold the metal lip and the three 5/0 treble hooks in place. The wire used for this construction is bent into a loop to form the eye in front of the lip and plug as shown in the illustration. To assemble this plug, first cut a slit at the head of the plug body to accept the metal lip, then drill a hole for the wire to run through the body. This hole is slightly off center at the head of the plug, but through the center at the tail. Two small holes drilled through the head and metal lip and two screws will hold the metal lip in place.

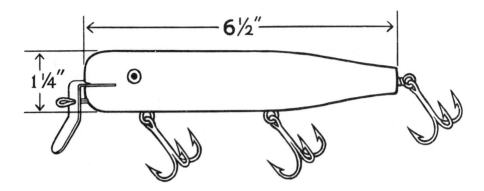

Swimming type surface plug.   *Figure 43.*

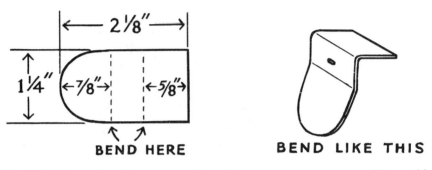

BEND HERE   BEND LIKE THIS

Metal lip for swimming type surface plug.   *Figure 44.*

Still another surface plug is the flaptail type with a revolving tail. This is shown in Fig. 45. It can have a body 6½ inches long and a diameter of 1⅛ inches. The tail tapers to about ⅝ inch and the head is cut slightly at a slant on top and rounded out a bit. This plug has a metal tail of the type and size shown in Fig. 46, cut out of sheet brass. To attach this tail to the plug, use a small metal bracket about 1¼ inches long and ¼ inch wide. This can also be cut from sheet brass. After it is cut out, it is bent about ⅜ inch from the end, after a hole has been drilled. A long brass wire nail is inserted in this hole. Before you do this, however, add a small brass nut or washer next to the head of the long nail to serve as a bearing. Then slip the metal tail on the nail and form an eye with pliers to hold the tail. Next, drill two holes in the bracket and fasten it with two small screws at the tail of the wooden plug body. The details showing how these parts are made are in Fig. 47. To finish off this plug, add two treble hooks at the belly and a screw eye at the nose to which you tie the fishing line.

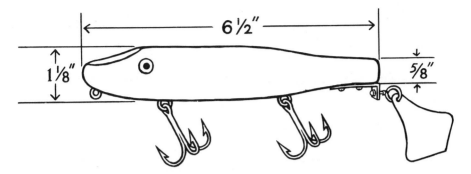

Figure 45.   *Flaptail surface plug.*

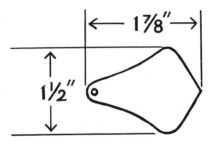

Figure 46.   *Metal flaptail.*

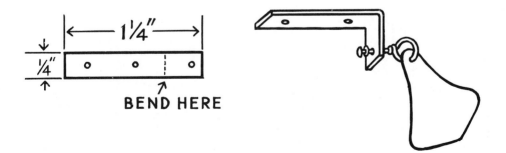

Figure 47.   *Metal bracket for holding flaptail.*

Another very effective saltwater fishing plug is the "torpedo" type shown in Fig. 48. This plug can be about 4½ inches long and ⅞ inch in diameter at its thickest part. It tapers at both ends and has two treble hooks in sizes No. 1/0 or 2/0, one attached at the tail and the other at the belly. A screw eye is attached to the nose for the fishing line.

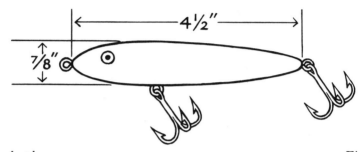

Torpedo plug.   *Figure 48.*

Saltwater anglers have also found the "darter" type plugs very effective for many fish. You can make a small one to use with light spinning or casting tackle in the same size as the freshwater darter shown in Fig. 11. But for the saltwater model you should use longer and stronger screw eyes and heavier wire hooks.

To make a larger darter plug for surf fishing or to use with heavy saltwater tackle, follow the dimensions shown in Fig. 49. The body can be 6½ inches long and an inch in diameter. The tail tapers to about ⅝ inch. The top of the plug slopes downward toward the nose,

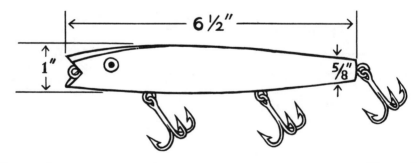

Darter plug.   *Figure 49.*

where there is a triangular cut or notch in front. A screw eye is screwed in this cut to hold the fishing line. Three treble hooks in size 5/0 are attached, two at the belly and one at the tail.

A large "wobbler" type plug suitable for surf fishing is shown in Fig. 50. It can have a body 7 inches long with a diameter of $1\frac{1}{8}$ inches at the head and tapering to about $\frac{5}{8}$ inch at the tail. The head is cut at a slant of forty-five degrees. This plug also carries three 5/0 treble hooks, two at the belly and one at the tail. A large screw eye at the head holds the fishing line.

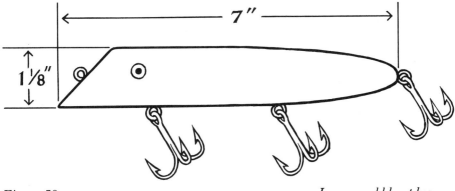

Figure 50.   *Large wobbler plug.*

Finally, we have the "underwater" plug shown in Fig. 51. This has a body 7 inches long and a diameter of $1\frac{3}{8}$ inches at its thickest part. It tapers sharply toward the head and more gradually toward

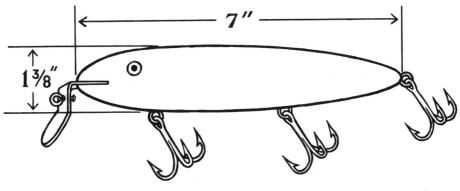

Figure 51.   *Underwater plug.*

the tail. This plug has a metal lip of the size and shape shown in Fig. 52. If you use the through-wire construction method all you have to do is bend the lip as shown and drill a hole for the wire loop that will form the eye.

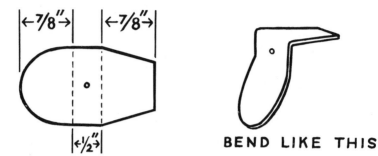

Metal lip for underwater plug.   *Figure 52.*

Another way to attach this lip is shown in Fig. 53. You make and bend the metal lip in the same way, but drill three holes as shown. Then get a long, brass wire nail, insert it into the single hole in the center of the lip, and bend the wire with round-nosed pliers to form an eye for the fishing line. To attach this lip to the plug body, cut a slit in the head of the plug to take the metal lip and drill two holes through the nose of the plug to meet the holes in the metal lip. Use two round-head brass screws to fasten the metal lip in place (see Fig. 54). This plug also takes three 5/0 treble hooks, two at the belly and one at the tail.

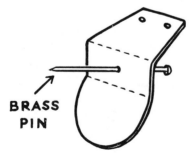

Forming an eye for the metal lip.   *Figure 53.*

SCREWS

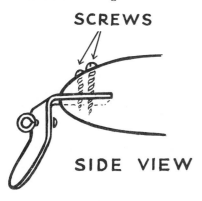

SIDE VIEW

SCREWS

TOP VIEW

Using screws to attach lip to plug.   *Figure 54.*

Saltwater plugs can be painted or sprayed in the same way as freshwater plugs, using the methods described in previous chapters. Choose any color combinations you like—you'll find the "blue mullet" finish one of the best. To get this finish, the plug is first painted or sprayed white, then a blue black is added blending into the white along the sides. Another popular saltwater combination is blue and silver, with the blue on the back and the silver along the sides. A silver scale finish can also be sprayed on. Or it can be a solid silver finish.

When making your saltwater plugs it is very important to use the best quality and strongest saltwater treble hooks you can obtain. Strong hooks are the only ones that will stand up any length of time in salt water. Light wire hooks are easily straightened out by big fish, and rust weakens them in a short time.

The basic saltwater plugs described above will take care of most fishing needs. But don't let that stop you from experimenting with different shapes, sizes, or weights. Although it is easier to duplicate existing models of plugs, more satisfaction is obtained if you design your own. And there is always a chance that it will turn out to be a better fish-getter than existing plugs on the market.

5

SPOONS

The spoon is one of the best lures the angler can use in fresh or salt-water fishing. It is compact and heavy enough to cast well, especially in the smaller sizes. It can be used when casting or trolling, and attracts all kinds of fish because of its brilliant "flash" and lively, swaying action.

The spoon is also one of the oldest fishing lures used by man, having its origins in the dim past. The lure we know as the modern "spoon" was used a long time ago in Scandinavian countries. In this country the spoon was developed and perfected in the early 1800s. The story goes that a fisherman named Julio T. Buel dropped a teaspoon into the water. As he watched it twist and turn it gave him an idea. He started experimenting and soldered a hook to the end of another teaspoon and attached his line to the handle, which was partly cut off. It caught fish and then he went into the business of making spoons for fishermen.

You can make a spoon lure of sorts by merely taking a teaspoon or tablespoon and cutting off the handle. Holes can be drilled at each end for holding the hook and line. Such a homemade spoon lure will catch fish, but is too deeply dished and the action is not the best. A much better spoon can be made by following the design shown in Fig. 55. This is one of the basic designs patterned after the famous "Dardevle" copied by many fishing tackle manufacturers.

To make a freshwater spoon from scratch you have to obtain brass or copper sheet metal in various thicknesses. The smaller-size spoons that run only from $1\frac{1}{2}$ to $2\frac{1}{2}$ inches in length use thinner-gauge metal than the larger spoons that measure from 3 to 5 inches in length.

This metal can be cut and filed out to the size desired, then bent

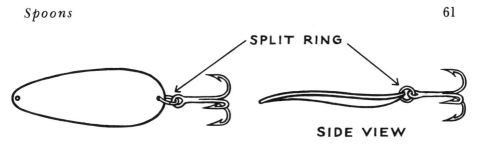

SPLIT RING

SIDE VIEW

Figure 55.   *Common type of fresh-water spoon.*

and hammered into the proper concave shape. This is a lot of work if done with hand tools and takes time even with the aid of power tools. Then the holes to take the hooks and line have to be drilled. If the hook is soldered to the spoon, that's another operation. Next, you have the spoons plated in nickel, chrome, gold, or silver. Or if you want to use the brass or copper finish of the original metal, you must polish or buff it.

Frankly, when one figures the time, energy, and money spent in making freshwater spoons from the raw material, it really doesn't pay—not unless one is willing to go to the expense of having a die made to stamp out the spoons on a punch press. Such a die runs into quite a bit of money, and unless you need hundreds or thousands of spoons it isn't worth it.

Fortunately, you don't have to go to the trouble of shaping your own freshwater spoons or spending money for expensive dies. Some of the mail-order houses listed in the back of this book carry spoons in various sizes, shapes, and weights. They are all complete with shiny gold, silver, chrome, brass, copper, or painted finishes and can be bought cheaply, especially in large quantities. You can buy a dozen of the spoons and the other parts such as split rings and hooks and then assemble the spoons in a matter of minutes.

Split rings come in different sizes; the smaller ones are used for small spoons while the larger ones are needed for the bigger spoons. They are usually made from spring steel or solid brass. The steel split rings are plated and are suitable for freshwater spoons, but for salt water the solid brass rings are better, since they do not rust.

Fig. 56 shows how to use a knife blade to spread a split ring apart so that it can be forced into the hole on the spoon. Once you have the split ring started, just keep turning it until it snaps on completely. You can put two split rings on most spoons, one in front for the fishing line and the other in the back, to which a treble hook is attached.

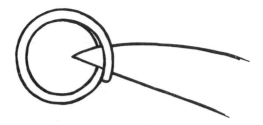

Figure 56.   *Using knife blade to open split ring.*

The treble hook can be plain or it can be wound with bucktail hair or feathers.

Although spoons with metal finishes are the most popular, you can paint them in various colors—such as all white, all yellow, or red and white stripes—if you want to do so. Usually only the convex side is painted, the concave side retaining the metal silver or nickel or chrome finish. You can also paint or spray the convex side with a natural fish-scale finish. For painting by hand with a brush, enamels are best. For spraying, use the quicker-drying lacquers. Clear lacquer or varnish can also be sprayed on a metal finish to keep it from tarnishing.

Although it really doesn't pay to cut or stamp out your own freshwater spoons, it's a different matter when we come to the larger saltwater spoons. These are more expensive and it often pays to make your own. Also, you cannot buy the larger metal spoon bodies already stamped out and plated as you can the smaller freshwater ones. So you have to either buy the completed spoon in a tackle store or make your own.

For pounding and shaping saltwater spoons you need a wooden anvil, which is nothing but a rectangular block of wood. Almost any block of hard wood such as oak or Douglas fir about 12 inches long and 5 or 6 inches thick is suitable. Toward one end of the block, drill a big hole and insert a peg of hard wood. You can also dig out some shallow holes and grooves along the working faces of the wood block (see Fig. 57). When shaping a spoon, lay the sheet metal on the peg or over the shallow holes and pound it with a wooden mallet (see Fig. 58).

As an aid in shaping the metal, make some punches out of hard wood. The sheet metal is placed over the hole or groove on the wood block and the punch is held at the spot where you want the metal to be formed. Then strike the wood punch with the mallet to shape the spoon.

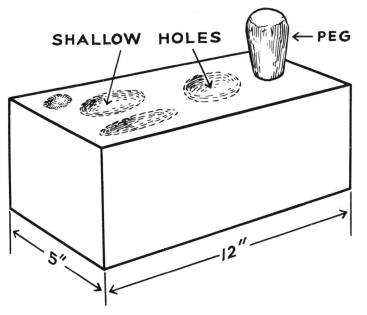

Figure 57.   *Wood block for shaping spoons.*

Figure 58.   *Using the wood block to shape a spoon.*

The metal for shaping spoons can be sheet brass, copper, or stainless steel. Stainless steel is being used more and more and is especially suitable for saltwater spoons because it doesn't corrode or tarnish. But stainless steel, especially in the heavier gauges, is very hard and springy and tough to cut and work with hand tools. If you have a workshop with power tools you can work with stainless steel. But if you do not have power tools and must use hand tools, you'll find it easier to work with brass, copper, or other soft metals.

Spring brass is a good metal, and if you obtain sheets of this material in $\frac{1}{32}$-inch thickness you'll be able to make varied sizes of spoons for saltwater fishing. Of course, somewhat lighter gauges can be used for the smaller spoons and heavier gauges are more suitable for the larger spoons. The metal used should have enough spring so that it doesn't bend out of shape too readily when a big fish is hooked.

The first step in making a spoon is to draw and cut out a pattern of the shape and size you want from a piece of cardboard or heavy paper. This way, all your spoons will be uniform in size and you won't have to make a new drawing to follow each time. Then trace the pattern outline on the sheet metal. The lighter gauges of brass or copper can be cut with ordinary hand snips and the heavier gauges can be usually handled with aviation snips. The duckbill snips are best for cutting the curves. You can also use a hacksaw or other type metal saw to remove excess metal. When cutting out the spoons the best procedure is to cut just outside the tracing a bit, leaving a narrow margin of metal. In other words, cut the spoon just a bit larger in size than the finished one will be. Then file the spoon down to the finished size.

The shape and size of the spoon will depend, of course, on the type of fishing you do, the weight desired, and the size of the fish to be caught. The blade can be long and narrow, bigger at the tail or at the head. It can be short and broad and rounded at both ends, or you can shape it like a fish, with two small fins and a tail. You can take almost any commercially made spoon and make a duplicate of it, or you can design your own. Fig. 59 shows some of the different shapes that can be used when making spoons.

Two basic types of spoons are usually made for saltwater fishing. One is based on the principle of the reverse S curve (see Fig. 60). Here the spoon is curved in one direction at the head and in the opposite direction at the tail. Both the head and tail are also hollowed or dished. The type of action you want will depend on how much of a curve you give the spoon. A spoon with a slight curve will have

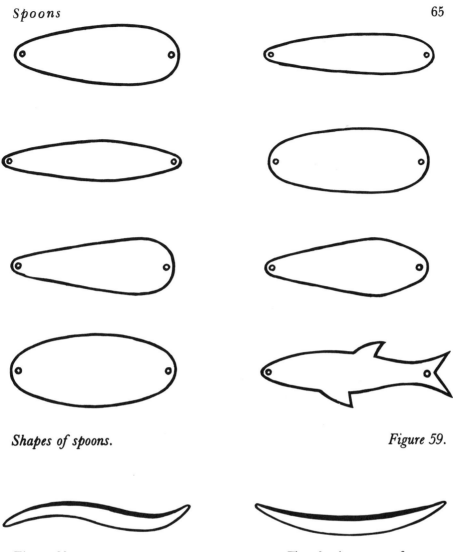

Shapes of spoons.

Figure 59.

Figure 60.

Two basic curves of spoons.

a somewhat faster wobble or wriggle than one that has extreme curves. The spoon with sharp curves and deep hollows will have more throw or sway when reeled or trolled. Naturally, experiments will show just how much to curve or dish a spoon. Before you shape too many spoons, try the first one out in the water to see if it has the desired action.

The other basic type of spoon is the more conventional shape shown in Fig. 60. Here the spoon is curved and dished both from the head to the tail and from side to side. This type is usually wider at the head and tapers toward the tail.

The size of the spoon will depend on the type of fishing you do and the fish you seek. Small spoons measuring only 3 or 4 inches long are best for casting and trolling for small, saltwater fish. These can also be of thicker gauge metal if you want to cast them. Medium-sized spoons from 4 to 8 inches can also be cast or trolled for bigger fish. Some of the biggest spoons made, such as the so-called bunker spoons, run up to 12 inches in length and are used for big fish such as striped bass.

The hook used on a saltwater spoon should be strong enough and heavy enough to hold big fish. A single hook is better than a treble hook.

There are various ways to attach the hook to a spoon. The easiest and quickest way is the method usually used on freshwater spoons, explained earlier. You drill one hole in the head and another in the tail and insert split rings. Then you slip a big single hook or treble hook on the split ring at the tail. Solid brass rings should be used for saltwater spoons, but since they are softer than spring steel, they should be soldered closed with a drop or two of lead.

Another strong way to attach a hook is to cut a slot in the tail end of the spoon and insert the hook shank through it. You also drill a small hole in the center of the spoon where the eye of the hook falls, then insert a small bolt through the hole and hook eye, and fasten it in place with a nut. This is shown in Fig. 61. The advantage of this method is that you can quickly remove an old rusted hook and replace it with a new one, if needed. For best results, use brass hardware to hold the hook.

If you use brass or copper sheet metal to make your spoons you can use them as they are by polishing them. A metal polish that can be bought in any hardware store can be used for this. How-

Figure 61.   Attaching hook to spoon.

ever, the most effective finish for saltwater is a nickel-plated or chrome-plated spoon. For plating, you can take the spoon to a shop that does metal plating, and do this before you assemble the spoons. Some anglers also paint their spoons silver, white, or yellow. Lacquers or enamel can be used for this. Of course, if you made your spoons from stainless steel all you have to do is polish them to a high gloss.

Naturally, homemade spoons may not look exactly like stamped-out commercial ones. There may be slight imperfections in the construction or the finish. But don't let that worry you. The fish don't know the difference if your spoon has the right action and will take them as readily as the ones bought in a fishing-tackle store.

6

SPINNERS

Somewhat similar to spoons are the spinners, which revolve on a wire shaft or swivel. They are also very effective lures for many fresh and saltwater fish, and an angler should always carry a good assortment of these lures. They are easy to make and very inexpensive when made at home.

Here again, it really doesn't pay to make the spinner blades themselves. The time and effort spent in cutting them out isn't worth it because you can buy all the spinner blades you want from many of the mail-order houses listed in the back of this book. They have them in stock in various shapes, sizes, and finishes and also carry the other parts needed such as wire, swivels, beads, clevises, body forms and weights, and split rings. You can buy the spinner blades by the dozen, gross, or even in thousand lots. In the larger quantities these blades are inexpensive and they are already stamped, shaped, and plated. You couldn't save much money by cutting out the blades yourself from sheet metal and then plating them. By buying the finished blades and other parts all you have to do is assemble the spinners.

Spinner blades come in various shapes such as the Indiana, Colorado, Willow Leaf, June Bug, Kidney, and Propeller types (see Fig. 62). They usually run in size from No. 00 to No. 7 and up. The lower the number, the smaller the blade. Numbers 00, 0, and 1 are small sizes suitable for trout and panfish, while the larger sizes are best for bass, pike, lake trout, and saltwater fish. You can get the spinner blades in various finishes such as gold, nickel, brass, and copper. Some are also made with hammered finishes. Still other blades are made from pearl or mussel shell.

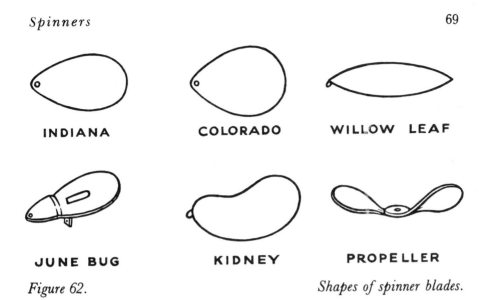

INDIANA   **COLORADO**   **WILLOW LEAF**

JUNE BUG   **KIDNEY**   **PROPELLER**

Figure 62.   *Shapes of spinner blades.*

To make completed spinners you also need spring-steel or stainless-steel wire for shafts. The spring-steel wire is usually coated with tin and is quite suitable for freshwater spinners. The stainless-steel wire is better for saltwater spinners. This wire is supplied in various diameters from .018 to .035, with the thin gauges being used for small spinners and the heavier gauges for the larger freshwater spinners and for saltwater types.

You also need beads, which are used on the wire shafts to act as bearings. These beads are made from different materials and come in different sizes. The light beads, made from pearl, glass, plastic, or hollow metal, are used for most spinners where no extra weight is required. The solid brass or metal beads are used for spinners that will be cast or for use in deep water. Instead of solid metal beads you can also use body forms made from metal to provide the weight (see Fig. 63). They can be ordered from fishing-lure-parts suppliers or you can make your own by obtaining solid

Figure 63.   *Metal body forms.*

brass rods, then cutting them into short lengths and drilling a hole through the center.

Spinners also require clevises that hold the blade so that it can revolve freely around the wire shaft. There are two main types as shown in Fig. 64. They usually come in two or three different sizes for small and large spinners.

Figure 64.   *Two types of clevises.*

Split rings are also needed in various sizes when making spinners. Barrel swivels such as those shown in Fig. 65 are also required in different sizes for some types of spinners. Some of the split rings and swivels can be bought in fishing-tackle stores, but you can save money if you buy them in larger quantities such as gross lots from a mail-order house.

Figure 65.   *Two types of barrel swivels.*

The basic spinner that can be used for trolling for many fish is the Indiana blade on a short wire shaft as shown in Fig. 66. To make this spinner cut off a length of wire for the shaft and form a locking-type eye on one end. For this you'll need diagonal cutting pliers and round-nosed pliers (the small jeweler's round-nosed pliers are best for this work). The first step in making the locking eye is to form it with the round-nosed pliers about an inch from the end of the wire shaft. Then form the catch part on the end of the wire (see Fig. 67 for the steps in doing this). Chapter 12 on leaders and connections will also give you tips on forming eyes and snaps that can be used when making spinners.

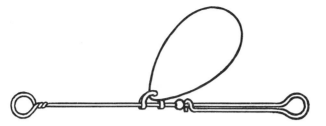

Basic type of spinner. *Figure 66.*

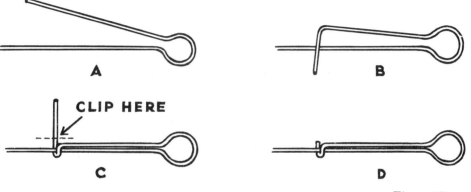

CLIP HERE

Forming a locking eye on shaft. *Figure 67.*

After you have finished the locking eye, slide about two metal or glass beads on the shaft, then add the spinner blade on a clevis and slide it up the wire shaft. To finish the spinner, form an eye on the end of the shaft to which the leader or line will be attached. The spinner is ready for use after you add a plain or feathered treble hook to the locking eye at the tail.

Another way to attach the hook to the spinner is to use a sliding coil spring or sleeve that slides on the shaft up to the eye and holds the wire together (see Fig. 68). These coil springs and brass or copper sleeves can be bought in various diameters from the mail-order houses. Still another way to attach a hook to a spinner is to form a permanent closed eye on the end of the wire, then slip on a split ring with a hook, as shown in Fig. 69.

These methods of attaching a hook to a spinner are used if you plan to change the hook often. If, however, you want to make a stronger permanent attachment, you merely form an eye on the end of the wire shaft, slip on the treble hook, and then close the eye for good.

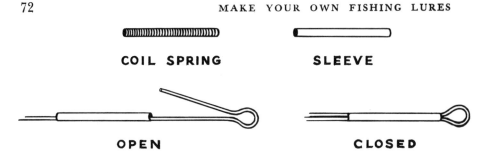

Figure 68.   *Using a coil spring or sleeve to close the eye on a shaft.*

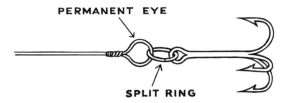

Figure 69.   *Permanent eye on a spinner shaft.*

The above basic spinner makes use of a single blade. If you want to add another blade to the shaft, use a slightly longer wire and after slipping on the first blade add a small metal bead that you then solder to the shaft above the first blade. Then slip on a loose bead or two and your second blade before forming the eye at the front of the wire shaft. This is shown in Fig. 70.

Another popular and effective spinner is the June Bug type shown in Fig. 71. The June Bug blade has an extension cut from

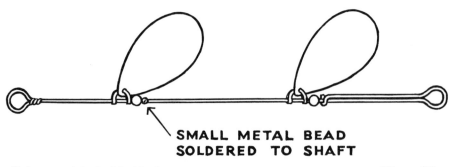

Spinner with double blade.   Figure 70.

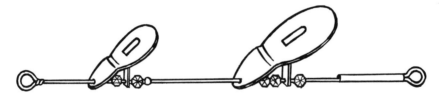

Single-blade June bug spinner.   *Figure 71.*

the blade itself, and this keeps the blade revolving at a fixed distance from the shaft. This spinner works very freely and smoothly even at slow speeds. When making this type of spinner use the large, red-ruby cut-glass beads as bearings on the shaft and add a barrel swivel at the front end of the spinner to which the line is tied. At the other end, attach a long-shank single hook such as the Carlisle pattern. Anglers usually use this spinner with the hook baited with a minnow, strip of fish, pork rind, or a gob of worms. You can also make this spinner with two blades using a longer wire shaft and adding a smaller blade up front as shown in Fig. 72.

The propeller type of spinner shown in Fig. 73 is also good to

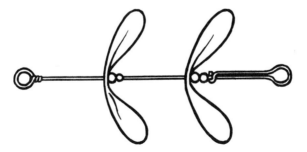

Double-blade June bug spinner.   *Figure 72.*

Figure 73.   *Propeller type spinner.*

use when trolling at slow speeds. You can buy the propeller blades in the larger sizes from the fishing-lure-parts suppliers. The two propeller blades used to make this spinner are spaced so that they revolve freely without interfering with each other. You have to solder a metal bead to the wire shaft to keep the first propeller blade away from the rear one. This type of spinner is usually used with a feathered treble hook attached behind it.

Another popular spinner is the type known as the "Cherry Bobber" or "Cherry Drifter," shown in in Fig. 74. This spinner makes use of a wooden, pear-shaped body that gives it buoyancy and prevents it from sinking too fast. You can make these bodies from any light wood, but balsa is preferred because it is easy to work. The wood body is then painted a bright red—a daylight florescent lacquer is best for this. Then fluorescent plastic beads are slipped on the wire shaft to act as bearings. A small treble hook is attached to the tail end of the spinner to complete it.

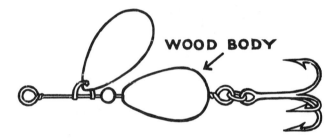

WOOD BODY

Figure 74.   *Cherry bobber spinner.*

Still another old-time favorite among spinners is the "Colorado," shown in Fig. 75. Here, instead of using a wire shaft, you use two barrel swivels and two split rings. The blade, which is the round-type Colorado, is attached to the split ring as shown. The split ring at the tail holds either two single hooks or one treble hook.

Most of the spinners above are used for trolling, but they can also be cast if you add a small clincher sinker or other weight to the leader. You can also get some sheet lead and cut out a small rudder that is then folded over the wire shaft of the spinner in front of the blade (see Fig. 76). To keep it from sliding down the shaft, make more turns with the wire than usual when forming the eye of the spinner. Then crimp the lead rudder on these turns

Figure 75.   *Colorado type spinner.*

Lead keel weight and its position in front of the spinner blade.   *Figure 76.*

with pliers. In addition to serving as a casting weight, the lead rudder also acts as a keel and helps prevent the spinner from twisting the line. You can paint this lead weight in any color you want and even add an eye on each side.

You can also make special casting or trolling weights that are detachable and can be added to the spinner at the front. (See chapter 13 on making sinkers for details on how such weights can be made.)

For easy casting, however, you can't beat the "French" type of spinner, shown in Fig. 77. These usually have short, wire shafts on which one or more heavy brass body weights are added. These body weights come in various shapes, sizes and designs, as shown in Fig. 63. French-type spinners also use a special heavier blade than the regular kinds of spinners. Both the body weights and the blades can be ordered from many of the supply houses. These spinners, which make excellent lures for casting, usually have a small treble hook attached.

French type spinner.   *Figure 77.*

Other casting-type spinners use heavy brass beads for body weight, as shown in Fig. 78. These beads come in different sizes and are usually arranged on the shaft, as shown in the illustration. You can also use lead body weights that come in bullet, torpedo, or double taper shapes (see Fig. 79). They have a center hole and come in different weights and sizes. You can order such lead weights either unpainted or painted.

Another way to make spinners is to use nylon leader material instead of wire to serve as a shaft. You can buy the nylon material

Spinner with solid metal beads.   *Figure 78.*

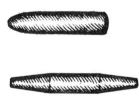

Figure 79.   *Lead weights for spinner bodies.*

in coils or spools of various diameters and strengths. Cut off a length, tie a loop for an eye up front, slip on the beads, plus a clevis with a blade, and then tie either a single hook or treble hook at the tail end. The larger glass or plastic beads are best for this type of spinner because they have bigger holes through which the nylon leader material can be threaded. If you want the spinner blade to revolve well above the hook, tie knots on the leader to act as stops against which the beads will rest. Fig. 80 shows different types of spinners that you can make using the nylon leader material. You can easily work out many of your own combinations.

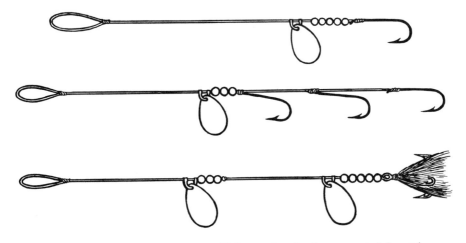

Figure 80.   *Using nylon leader material for spinners.*

The saltwater-type spinners are very similar to the freshwater ones described above. In fact, you can use many of the freshwater types for salt water if you use heavier wire shafts, bigger blades, and stronger hooks.

One special kind of saltwater spinner is the "willow leaf" type, shown in Fig. 81. To make this spinner you will have to cut out and shape your own blades since they can be bought finished only in the smaller sizes. For saltwater fishing the willow leaf blade should be at least 2¾ inches long and ⅝ inch wide. This spinner also has an extension like the June Bug spinner described earlier. This can be soldered to the blade at a fixed distance from the shaft. And instead of a clevis the blade is bent in front and a hole is drilled. Another hole is drilled in the extension arm and the wire

Willow leaf salt-water spinner.   *Figure 81.*

shaft is then slipped through both holes. If you use stainless steel to make the blade you don't have to plate it, but merely polish it.

When making this spinner or any other saltwater type, use heavier wire for the shaft. When attaching the hook or swivel at the front or rear of the shaft, form a permanent eye, which is strongest. However, if you plan to change hooks or swivels you can form a locking snap or clasp-type loop, as shown in Fig. 82. Full instructions for forming such a snap can be found in chapter 14 on making leaders and connections.

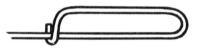

Locking snap on salt-water spinner.   *Figure 82.*

The willow leaf spinner usually has a gang of two or three hooks attached behind it, and these are baited with a whole bait-fish, worms, a strip of pork rind, or squid.

Another saltwater spinner is the "fluke" spinner shown in Fig. 83. A pair of Colorado-type blades are used to make this spinner, mounting them on a heavy wire shaft with big glass or plastic beads. A single long-shank Carlisle hook is attached behind the blades, and this is baited with a live killifish or other saltwater minnow.

Fluke spinner.   *Figure 83.*

A somewhat similar spinner, which makes use of smaller Indiana-type blades, is the "snapper" shown in Fig. 84. This also has an extra long-shanked hook attached at the rear.

Snapper spinner.   *Figure 84.*

The spinners described and illustrated above do not cover every type made or used. But they are the basic types from which you can go on and make endless combinations of your own.

7

JIGS

One of the deadliest lures used in saltwater fishing is the jig. It is also very popular and effective now for freshwater fishing. This lure, which consists of a metal "head" in which a single hook is embedded, also has a "body" or "skirt" of bucktail hair, feathers, nylon, plastic, or other material. The entire combination makes a small, compact lure heavy enough to cast well. Whether cast or trolled or jigged up and down near the bottom, it is very attractive to almost every fish that swims. In fact, if I had to choose but a single artificial lure for saltwater fishing, I'd not hesitate an instant to pick a good assortment of jigs in different sizes, weights, and colors. And the jig is also a versatile lure to use for freshwater fishing. Obviously, the fresh or saltwater angler who wants to catch fish should carry an assortment of jigs in his tackle box or bag.

For best results, you need a wide variety of jigs in different sizes, colors, materials, and weights. You also need many replacements for those jigs which are lost when they get caught on the bottom or are broken off by a fish. So you can save quite a bit of money and have a lot of fun making your own jigs. They are very easy to make once you know how, and I am surprised more fresh and saltwater anglers don't mold their own jigs.

To make jigs you need some kind of mold. A simple and inexpensive temporary mold can be made from several kinds of materials, the cheapest and most popular being plaster of Paris. This white powder can be bought in any paint or hardware store and is mixed with water. A five- or ten-pound bag of the stuff costs very little and will make several molds.

Somewhat similar but a bit more expensive are "water putty" and "crack filler" mixtures, which also come in powder form in containers and are mixed with water. Most hardware or paint stores carry these. Another material that can be used is "iron paste" or "iron cement," which comes in powdered form too. You also add water to make a heavy paste for pouring the mold. Most hardware stores carry it.

There are also many kinds of dental cements and plasters that can be used to make temporary molds. Ask your dentist to suggest one or two of these. Or you can go to a dental supply house and ask for such a cement.

The first step in making a jig mold is to obtain a pattern that can be copied. For this you can buy a finished jig you like and want to duplicate in a fishing tackle store. Then remove the hair or feathers or nylon dressing and file off the hook close to the jig head.

You can also fashion your own jig by using a soft wood to carve out a pattern. In fact, almost any wood can be used to carve out a pattern, but the softer woods are easier to work with. Other substances suitable for making patterns are plastic, wax, soap, and modeling clay. If you use wood for a pattern, sandpaper it smooth when finished and varnish or shellac it to waterproof it and give it a smooth finish. Fig. 85 shows some basic jig heads that can be copied when making a pattern.

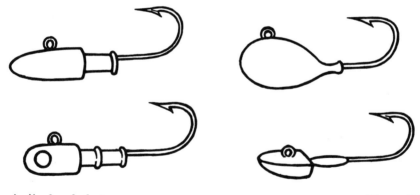

Basic jig head shapes.   *Figure 85.*

After you have the jig pattern, you are ready to make the mold. For this you need a small container such as a cardboard box about 3 inches long, 2 inches wide, and about 1½ inches deep. If you can't obtain a suitable box, you can make one, using heavy cardboard or thin sections of wood. Cut out the four sides to form a box and place them on a flat surface such as glass or metal. Then anchor the box in place using Scotch tape at the corners and sides. Modeling clay can also be used to hold the box sides to the metal or glass base (see Fig. 86).

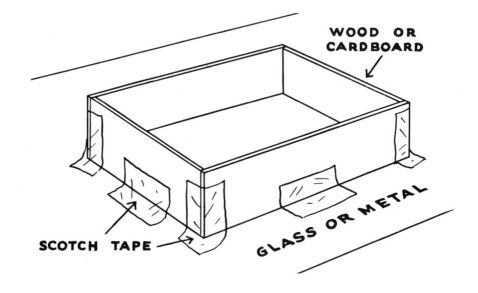

WOOD OR CARDBOARD

SCOTCH TAPE

GLASS OR METAL

Making a box from wood or heavy cardboard.   *Figure 86.*

The next step is to coat the inside of the box and the jig pattern itself with petroleum jelly to prevent the plaster from sticking. A thin coat is all that is necessary. Now mix some of the plaster of Paris or water putty in a container with water. You can do this with a stick, but your hands are much better for feeling and breaking up any lumps. Keep adding water and plaster until you get a heavy consistency—one that still pours freely, however. And be sure you make enough to fill the box half full.

Now pour this plaster into the small box until it is half full. Then sink your jig pattern halfway into the wet plaster. You should allow a space of about ⅜ inch between the rear end of the jig and the box side and 1½ inches from the opposite end of the box side to the jig (see Fig. 87).

Next, sink two flat-headed nails into the wet plaster, allowing about ¼ inch of the pointed ends to protrude. They can be placed

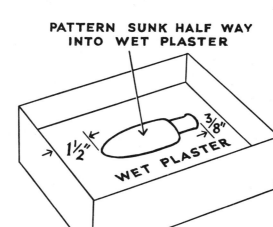

PATTERN SUNK HALF WAY INTO WET PLASTER

Figure 87.   *Position of jig pattern in mold box.*

diagonally opposite near the corners. They will act as locating pins when using the two mold halves while pouring the jig (see Fig. 88).

You now have half the mold completed and must wait until the plaster sets before you pour the other half. When it hardens (usually in about an hour or so), coat the entire surface of the plaster cast and inside of the box with petroleum jelly or a heavy oil. After this, mix more plaster of Paris or whatever substance you are using to make the mold. Then fill the box to the top with this mixture.

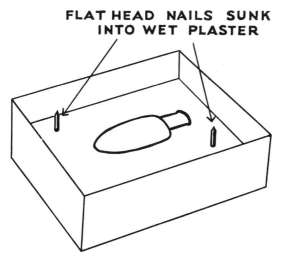

FLAT HEAD NAILS SUNK INTO WET PLASTER

Figure 88.   *Position of nails which act as location pins.*

After this second pouring of plaster sets, in an hour or so, you break apart the box holding the cast. Then separate the two halves of the mold with a knife blade, as shown in Fig. 89. This must be done with care in order not to break off any section of the plaster mold. You'll notice a line indicating where the two halves meet, and by slowly working a knife blade between them at several points you can usually separate them with no trouble. The original pattern will be found adhering to one of the halves and this must be worked loose very carefully so you don't damage the edge. You will then have two damp plaster halves as shown in Fig. 90. Set them aside to dry and

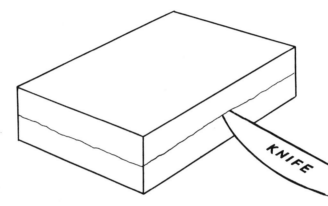

Using knife to separate halves of mold.   *Figure 89.*

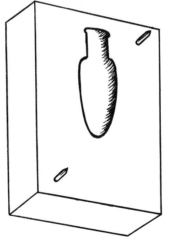

Plaster mold, separated.   *Figure 90.*

season for about two weeks. This is important because if you try to pour the hot metal into a damp mold it will spatter all over or will crack the mold.

When the mold has dried thoroughly cut out eyelet grooves and hook slots as well as a pouring hole. First you must get samples of the hook size and wire eyelets you will be using. The eyelets are easily formed from soft copper or brass wire in the shape shown in Fig. 91. When you have made the simple eyelet and have the hook you

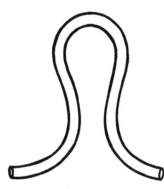

Figure 91.   *Shape of wire eye.*

will use, place them in position on the plaster mold and trace around them with a pencil to indicate the part of the mold that will have to be cut out. Wood-carving tools are ideal for removing this plaster to make room for the eyelet and hook, but you can also use a small, pointed knife. A larger knife can be used to carve out the funnel-shaped pouring hole. This is done to both halves of the plaster mold as shown in Fig. 92.

For casting the jigs you will need some lead or block tin or a combination of the two, such as bar solder. Scrap lead or tin can be bought from a junk dealer or a plumber. Solder bars are sold by plumber's supply houses or hardware stores. The greater the proportion of tin you use, the lighter the jig will be both in weight and appearance. A jig cast from pure tin will be very white and silvery in appearance and does not have to be painted. A jig cast from lead will be darker and will turn almost black later. Such jigs are heavier and are usually painted.

Melt the lead or tin in an iron ladle over a gas range or electric

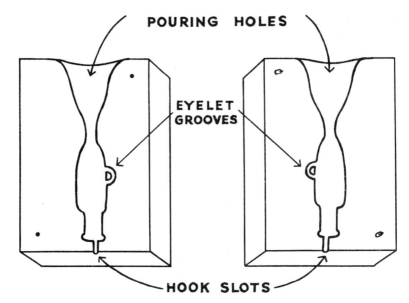

POURING HOLES

EYELET GROOVES

HOOK SLOTS

Figure 92.   *Plaster halves of mold prepared for wire eye and hook.*

stove. Before putting the two plaster mold halves together, pour some of the hot metal into each half to warm it, or place the plaster mold close to the flame or heat to make it warm. The next step is to place the wire eyelet and the hook in the groove and slot (see Fig. 93). Then put the two halves together, hold them with the pouring hole up, and pour the molten metal as quickly as possible right up to the top of the pouring hole (see Fig. 94).

When you notice the hot metal harden you can lay the mold on its side to cool off a bit. After the first jig is poured you'll usually need a glove or rag to hold the mold for subsequent pourings. It gets pretty hot, and unless the plaster mold is very thick you won't be able to hold it in your bare hand. If you want, you can grip the two plaster halves together with a C-clamp and hold the clamp to keep your hand from being burned.

After about a minute, depending on the size of the jig, you can separate the mold and take out the jig. It should be perfectly formed with no bad spots. If it isn't perfect, the lead or tin wasn't hot enough or the mold was too cool. After a little experimenting you'll be able to tell just how hot the molten metal must be to pour right. For best results, pour when the lead or tin has a bluish or purplish color on top. Every so often it's a good idea to scrape the scum off the surface of the lead in the ladle.

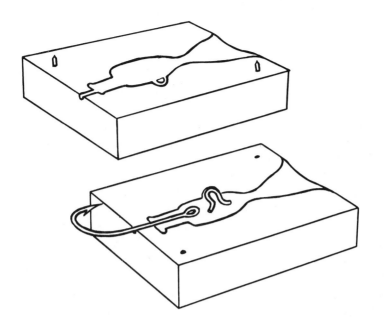

Hook and wire eye in place.   *Figure 93.*

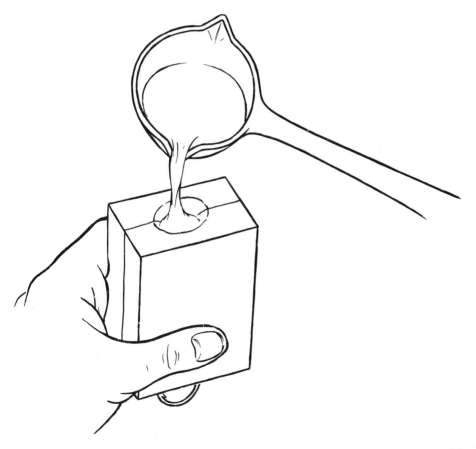

Figure 94.   *Pouring molten metal into the plaster mold.*

As you pour the jigs, keep cutting off the excess lead left at the pour hole with diagonal pliers and add it to the molten metal in the ladle. Once you start pouring it's best to continue until you have poured enough jigs for your needs. If you have two or three molds you can alternate between them to make different-sized jigs at the same time.

You can save time by designing your mold so that it takes the special jig hook shown in Fig. 95. Then you don't have to use a separate wire eyelet and hook. The bend in the hook makes it possible to cast it in a jig so that it serves both purposes. These special jig hooks are now available from most hook manufacturers and mail-order supply houses. These hooks come in light wire patterns that are best for freshwater fishing, and also in heavier wire patterns such as the O'Shaughnessy, which are used for salt water. Naturally, the size of the hook you use will also depend on the size of the jig and the fish you are after. The small hooks are used for the light jigs and freshwater fishing, while the bigger hooks are for the heavier jigs and saltwater fishing.

Special jig hook.   *Figure 95.*

A mold made from plaster of Paris or water putty is generally good for casting about a dozen or two dozen jigs before it breaks up. Small chips or holes in the plaster mold can be patched up with wet plaster or water putty. When doing this, make sure you wet the section of the mold to be filled before applying the liquid plaster. But if the mold breaks up too badly it's better to make a new one.

If you do a lot of fishing and need many jigs you can easily make a permanent mold that will last for years. All you do is go through the same steps in making the plaster halves. When the plaster mold is dry you carve out the groove and slot for the hook as well as the pouring hole and then send both halves to a foundry and have them copied in bronze. When you get the bronze halves back you must smooth the inside or the cavity with emery cloth. The bronze mold can be held together with a C-clamp for pouring. Or, if you have the tools, you can tap holes in both sections of the bronze mold and add a hinge and handles.

You can also buy ready-made metal molds complete with handles, to make different types, sizes, and weights of jigs, from some of the mail-order houses listed in the back of this book. When one takes into consideration how many thousands of jigs they will turn out over the years they are well worth the cost. In fact, it is often cheaper to buy one of these ready-made molds than to bother making your own permanent metal mold, unless, of course, you have a special jig design you want to make. Then the best idea is to make up a few of these jigs, using a plaster mold. If they turn out to be satisfactory you can then have a permanent mold made at the foundry. But for occasional fishing trips you can usually make all the jigs you need with a plaster mold.

After the jigs are poured they require some finishing. A metal mold usually pours more perfect jigs than a plaster-type mold, but even these still require some work. Most of the excess metal can be clipped off with cutting pliers or with a knife, and a file can be used to remove the rest. Then give the jig a smooth finish by rubbing it with fine steel wool. If it is made from tin you can also buff it or polish it.

The final step is to tie on a body or skirt of bucktail hair, feathers, or nylon. Bucktail hair and feathers can usually be bought in small packages in most fishing tackle stores or you can send away for these materials to a fly-tying supply house. You can save money by buying a whole bucktail. The natural bucktail is white and brown. You can use the white hair both for fresh and saltwater jigs, and some of the brown hair for freshwater jigs. Yellow bucktail is also popular for all kinds of fishing, and many other colors are available. You can also buy the white bucktail and dye it yourself. All-white and all-yellow jigs are the most popular both for fresh and saltwater fishing, but when tying the jigs you can blend several colors to imitate minnows or baitfish.

When tying bucktail hair around the jig head, do it in stages. The first step is to get some heavy silk, nylon, or linen thread. You can also use the heavier button cord or sewing thread if you want. White is the best color to use unless you want to match the head or hair of the jig with the same color. Cut off about a two-foot length of this thread, wrap a few turns of the thread around the jig head where the bucktail will go, and cover this wrapping with clear, quick-drying cement. Now quickly take a pinch of hair, lay it against the cement, and wrap a few turns of the thread around it (see Fig. 96). Then add another drop or two of cement, lay another pinch of hair against it, and tie a few more turns of thread around the hair. Keep doing this until you build up a thick body of hair around the hook, concealing most of it except the point and the barb (see Fig. 97). It is a good idea to make up several pinches of hair in advance and lay them on the table to be used as needed.

When you have the full amount of bucktail hair wound on the jig head, finish the job by wrapping the rest of the thread as tightly as possible over the jig. Then end it by tying a series of half-hitches. Finally, cover the thread wrapping with a heavy coat of clear, quick-drying cement.

Instead of bucktail hair you can use feathers of various colors on the jig (see Fig. 97). Neck or saddle hackle feathers are best

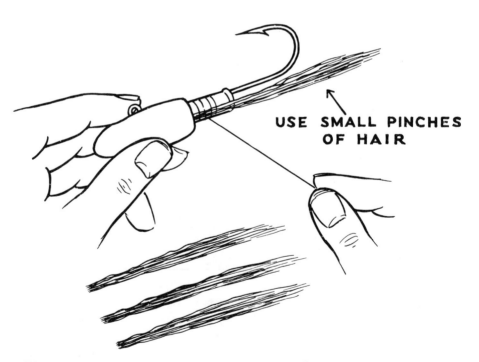

USE SMALL PINCHES OF HAIR

Figure 96.   *Winding hair on jig head.*

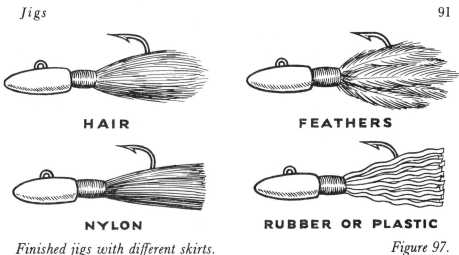

HAIR **FEATHERS**

NYLON **RUBBER OR PLASTIC**

Finished jigs with different skirts. *Figure 97.*

for this. Although various colors of feathers are used, white and yellow are the most popular for both fresh and saltwater fishing.

Nylon can also be used on a jig in various colors and lengths. It comes in the natural translucent color in different diameters and lengths and can be dyed other colors. The small diameters and lengths are best for small jigs, especially those used in freshwater fishing, and the thicker diameters and longer lengths are used for the larger saltwater jigs. When tying the nylon to the jig great care must be taken to do this as tightly as possible, because this material has a tendency to slip out from under the wrapping. For best results try to get the "crimped" nylon, which holds better than the smooth kind.

The final step in making jigs is to paint the metal head in whatever color you prefer. Of course, the jigs cast from pure tin or an alloy that is mostly tin can be left unpainted. The silvery appearance is attractive to many fishes. However, if you cast your jigs from lead you'll have to paint them, since the lead turns black and unattractive. You can use lacquer, enamel, or special paints such as the celluloid enamels. If white bucktail, feathers, or nylon was used for the body, you can paint the head white. If yellow was used, you can paint the head yellow, and so on. But combinations of different colors can also be tried.

To finish off the jigs many anglers also paint on a pair of eyes. These are not necessary to catch fish but they do give the jigs a professional look. Paint the eyes with a small, pointed brush or use the nail-dipping method described in chapter 2 on freshwater plugs.

Most jigs range in weight from $\frac{1}{8}$ to about 2 ounces. The smaller ones are best for freshwater fishing and for casting with light outfits. The heavier ones are more suited for saltwater fishing, trolling, and casting with heavy fishing tackle.

Jigs are so easy and inexpensive to make that every fresh and saltwater angler should make molds or buy molds to turn out a good supply and assortment of these lures to be prepared for the fishing season.

8

PLASTIC WORMS AND LURES

In recent years plastic worms and other plastic lures have become very popular for both fresh and saltwater fishing, and many anglers are beginning to make such lures at home or in their workshops. You can easily make hundreds of plastic worms or other plastic lures at little cost and have fun doing it.

The first step is similar to that described in chapter 7 on making jigs. You construct a small box about a half inch longer on each end than the worm you want to copy. This box can be made of heavy cardboard or thin wood sides as for jigs. You can also form a box of sorts with aluminum foil but this won't be as neat as a box made from cardboard or wood.

When the box is ready you mix some plaster of Paris and pour it into the box until it is about half full. Then you take a plastic worm you want to copy and press the worm into the wet plaster of Paris so that one-half of the worm is buried. The worm should be placed so that there's a half-inch of plaster in front of the head and a similar distance from the tip of tail to the edge of the box (see Fig. 98).

Then wait until the plaster of Paris has set and coat the entire mold itself with petroleum jelly. This will help prevent the sticking of the upper half of the mold to the bottom half and make it easier to separate the two halves. Now mix some more plaster of Paris and pour it into the box to form the second half of the mold.

When this new pouring has set and hardened you can separate the two halves with a knife by working all around it (the same way as shown and described in the previous chapter on making jigs). Now use the knife blade to carve a pouring hole in both halves through which the plastic will be poured.

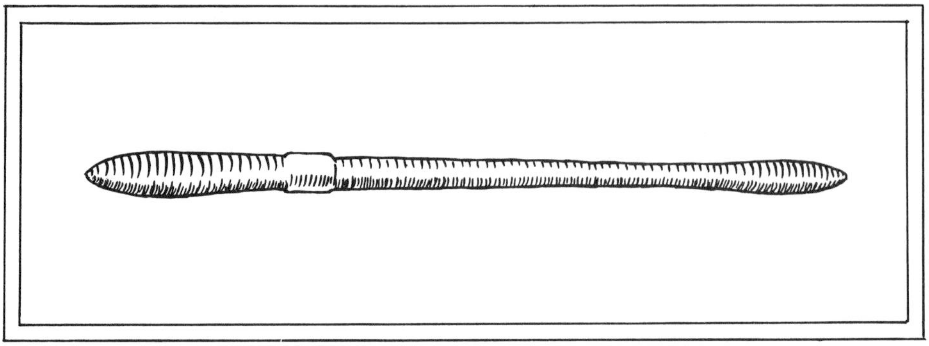

Figure   98.   *Placing worm in box.*

Before using, let the plaster of Paris dry for a few days. You can speed this up if you want by baking the mold in an oven for a while. When the mold is dry get some white epoxy paint and coat the worm cavity in both halves with it. This coating will produce worms with a shiny, smooth appearance. If the epoxy paint is not used the worms will be dull. After the paint dries in a day or two the mold is ready to use.

First coat the worm cavity with a light coat of petroleum jelly to keep the plastic from sticking to the mold when you want to remove the finished worm. You can hold the two halves in your hand when pouring or you can use rubber bands or clamps to hold them together.

If you have a lot of old plastic worms of the same color on hand you can melt these on a stove and pour the hot liquid into the mold. If not, you'll have to obtain the plastic that comes in cans in pints or gallons and can be obtained from some of the mail-order houses listed in the back of this book. Get the type of plastic that can be heated and is poured hot into a cold mold.

When the plastic is hot enough it should be poured into the mold and the mold should be held upright for two or three minutes. Then separate the halves and remove the worm and put it into a pan of cold water. You can add ice cubes to this water to make it even colder. The worm can then be removed from the water and is ready to be used.

You can make the same type of mold from plaster to form various other kinds of freshwater baits such as frogs, crayfish, lizards or salamanders, and minnows. For this you can copy the actual bait itself such as a real frog and use it as the model, or you can buy one of these baits already made from plastic and use that as the pattern.

And you can also buy ready-made molds for making plastic worms and other lures from some of the mail-order houses. These are cheap in price and most of them have two or three cavities so that you can make that many lures at the same time. These molds are made from aluminum, silicone rubber, or other materials, and most of them have to be heated on a stove before the plastic is poured. But there are plastics that can be heated and poured into cold molds. Most of these ready-made molds are the open-face type or just one half with grooves or cavities (see Fig. 99).

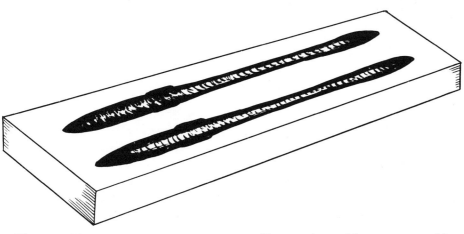

Figure 99. *Two-cavity rubber-worm mold.*

The basic process with a metal or aluminum mold is to first heat the mold. The best way to do this is to use an aluminum baking pan or griddle or cookie sheet and place it over a low stove flame. Then place the mold on one of these and heat it to a temperature of 350 degrees. Now pour the liquid plastic into the mold cavities until they are filled but not overfilled. The best way to do this is with a plastic squeeze bottle, especially if you are making fine-detailed baits such as crayfish, insects, or similar lures, but it can be used for making all baits (see Fig. 100).

Now watch the poured plastic for curing, which can be detected by the darkening of the plastic along the edges of the mold.

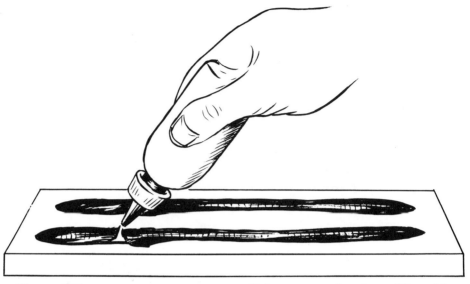

Figure 100.   *Using squeeze bottle to fill mold.*

Then place the mold in a pan of cold water for a few minutes for the plastic to harden. After this you can lift the plastic bait out of the cavity.

Plastic worms or other plastic lures can be made in one solid color such as white, yellow, red, orange, green, blue, or purple, or you can make different color combinations by adding the various colors to different parts of the mold.

The silicone rubber or flexible molds are superior to the metal ones in that they are easier and faster to use and you get better finished lures. Here you heat the liquid vinyl plastic to 350 degrees and stir it until it thickens and then pour it into the flexible mold. It is important to control this heat to the proper temperature, so you have to use a stove that can be set at 350 degrees. Then after the plastic has been poured into the mold, wait a minute or two and put the mold into a pan of water to cool.

Since the rubber molds are flexible they result in more rounded lures even when you use an open-face-type mold. The edges may overlap the cavity but the poured lures can still be removed from the mold with no trouble. Some of the mail-order houses listed in the back of this book sell such flexible molds and the liquid plastics to be used with them and also furnish instructions on how to use their molds.

When it comes to making saltwater plastic lures you shouldn't have much trouble making the smaller kinds, but may run into difficulties when making the bigger lures. The molds have to be much larger and more plastic is used. However, you can make molds to simulate the smaller mullet, balao or ballyhoo, herring, sardines, and eels.

You can make eels in various sizes and lengths the same way you make the worms with plaster of Paris casts. Then they can be rigged with one or two hooks in much the same manner as natural eels are rigged and which is described in chapter 11. Or you can rig them with a small metal squid to give them weight and action, also described in the same chapter. They can also be made in various colors, but for saltwater fishing the all-white, brown, purple, and black colors work best.

Another lure that has become a great fish "killer" in both fresh and saltwater is the plastic tail lure. This simple lure is actually a combination of a lead head jig and the short tail of a plastic worm

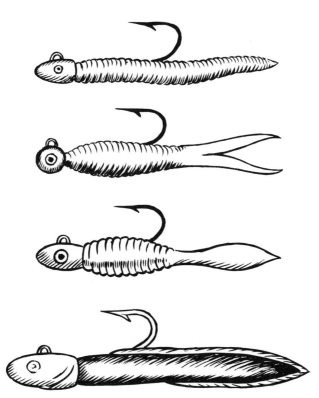

Figure 101.   *Plastic tail lures.*

or eel. These tails are easily made by using much the same methods and procedures as described in chapter 7 on making jigs and chapter 8 on making plastic worms. In fact, you can use the same molds to make the jigs and then use the molds made for plastic worms and then combine the two parts to make the tail lure.

Of course, you don't have to pour the entire plastic worm if you don't want to. You can just pour about three inches of the tail section. But you may want to make up special molds to pour the tails in actual lengths with no waste. The tail lures can be made in different sizes and weights and lengths using the big heavy jig heads and large hooks and large tails up to four or five inches in length for big saltwater fish. Or you can make the shorter, lighter jigs with small hooks and a tail only two inches long for small freshwater fish. (See Fig. 101 for some of the different types of tail lures that can be made.) You can buy some of these bait tails already made and copy them with your own molds.

9

METAL SQUIDS

Metal squids have been used by many saltwater fishermen from way back and are especially popular for surf fishing. They can also be used for casting and trolling from a boat in salt water. Metal squids come in various sizes and weights and in general look somewhat like a small boat with a V-shaped keel. Long and narrow squids are called sand-eel squids because they resemble this saltwater baitfish. Others are shorter and somewhat broader and simulate various baitfish such as spearing or silversides, smelt, and similar saltwater minnows. Still other metal squids are broad and deep and resemble mullet, herring menhaden, anchovies, and other fish of the herring family.

You'll find metal squids for sale in the fishing tackle stores near the ocean, especially along the Atlantic and Pacific coasts. You can buy one of these and make a mold from it. All you have to do beforehand is file off the hook and fill the hole where the line is attached with clay or wax or some other filler.

But quite a few anglers like to design their own metal squids and this can be done by carving a pattern from soft wood, plastic wax, or some similar substance. I've used balsa wood with great success. This soft wood is very easy to work and the only thing to do after you have finished the pattern is to varnish or shellac it to waterproof it and to give it a harder and smoother finish. Some of the basic types of metal squids that you can duplicate when making your own pattern are shown in Fig. 102. The methods used in making the molds and casting metal squids are quite similar to those described in chapter 7 on making jigs. There are some differences, however, so I will describe the procedure step by step.

After you have the pattern to be copied, get a small cardboard

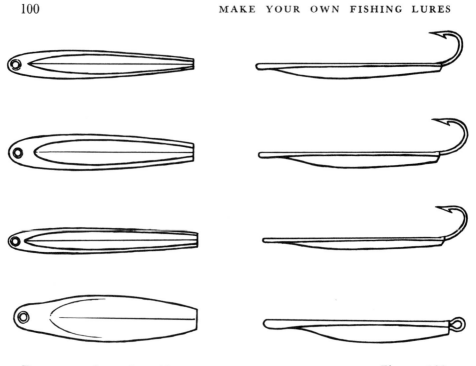

Four types of metal squids.   *Figure 102.*

box or make one out of wood or cardboard. It should be about 5 or 6 inches long, 2 inches wide, and 1¼ inches deep, but it can be bigger or smaller depending on the size of the squid to be made. You'll often find that the long and narrow cardboard boxes that are used to hold fishing plugs are ideal for this, but if you can't find the right box make a wood frame and anchor this to the plate of glass or a flat piece of metal. Scotch tape or modeling clay can be used to hold the sides of the box together and hold them on the base. This box or frame should be long enough and wide enough to clear the pattern or metal squid to be copied.

The next step is to coat the inside of the box or frame and the base with petroleum jelly. Then do the same thing with the pattern, leaving a thin coat of the grease so that the plaster won't stick to it. Now place the metal squid or pattern to be copied inside the box or frame with the flat part down and the keel up. Make certain that the tail end of the squid (where the hook was or will be) is only about ¼ inch away from the end of the box or frame (see Fig. 103).

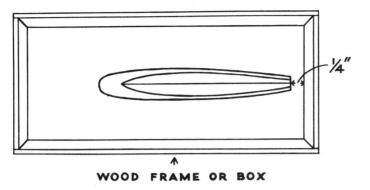

WOOD FRAME OR BOX

Metal squid pattern ready to be cast. *Figure 103.*

To make a temporary mold, use any of the materials such as plaster of Paris, water putty, or crack filler mentioned in the chapter on jigs. Mix the plaster or water putty with water and feel around with your hands to break up any lumps. This is important, or else the cast will be imperfect. Now pour the plaster into the box or frame until it covers the metal squid or pattern by at least ¾ inch. If the box is only about an inch or slightly more in depth, fill it with plaster up to the top. After pouring the plaster, wait about an hour before breaking up the box or frame apart. Turn the plaster cast over and remove the metal squid or pattern. This is best done with a sharp, pointed knife and prying under the pattern at the head to loosen it from the plaster. You may also have to cut a thin line all around the pattern with the knife if the plaster covered the pattern to any extent. It will now take about a week or a bit longer for the plaster mold to season and dry before it can be used.

In the meantime you can make a cover for the mold. This can be done by pouring another part in a box with plaster or water putty to make a flat, thick cover. You'll get somewhat better results, however, if you use a metal plate almost as wide and as long as the plaster cast for a cover. It can be made of brass, copper, or other metal and be from ⅛ to ¼ inch thick.

After the plaster mold is thoroughly dry, carve both a pouring hole at the head and a slot for the hook at the rear. Now take the metal plate that will be used as a cover and file a small triangular notch at one end that fits around the hook. (See Fig. 104 for an illustration of the finished plaster mold and the metal plate cover.)

Next you need some 6/0, 7/0 or 8/0 O'Shaughnessy hooks, de-

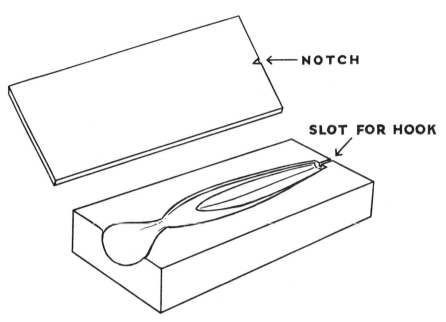

Figure 104.   Finished plaster mold and its metal cover.

pending on the size of the metal squid in your mold. For small squids
the 6/0 or even a 5/0 hook can be used, while for the larger squids
a 7/0 or 8/0 hook is better. When cutting the slot in the plaster mold,
make sure the correct-size hook is used as a sample. It must fit snugly into this slot (see Fig. 105).

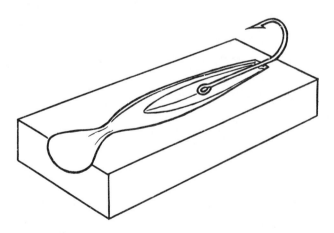

Hook fitted into slot of mold.   Figure 105.

You will need a fairly large C-clamp to hold the metal cover against the plaster mold while pouring. And it's a good idea to make a small wooden base where the mold will rest while you are setting it up and after you finish pouring the molten metal into it. This wooden base and the plaster mold all ready for pouring are shown in Fig. 106.

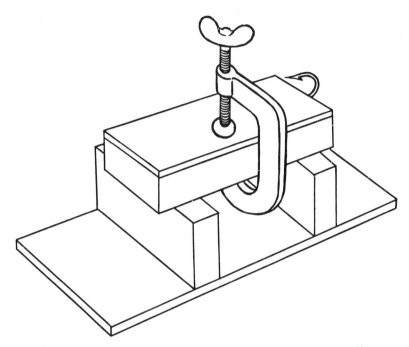

Clamped plaster mold, on wood base.   *Figure 106.*

Block tin with a small percentage of lead added should be used for pouring metal squids. Block tin can be obtained at times from a junk dealer who handles scrap metals. Used alone, it has a tendency to crack easily, but adding some lead will make it more flexible and easier to bend without cracking. Bar solder used by plumbers also contains block tin but most mixtures have too much lead and must be mixed with pure tin to get a metal squid with a white silvery finish.

However, block tin has become scarce and very expensive in recent years and you may find that you will have to pour your squids with lead. Then they will have to be plated or painted because lead turns black and is unattractive. One trick is to use a spray can with silver or aluminum paint and spray your lead squid with this to give it a more silvery appearance. Even though this silver color will crack or peel, in time you can always renew it in a matter of seconds by spraying it again.

It will be remembered that molds made from plaster of Paris or water putty have a short life and usually last just long enough to pour about two or three dozen squids. Then they chip up or crumble from the heat and a new mold must be made. If you make the mold from one of the dental cements it will last longer.

But if you want to make a permanent mold for casting metal squids, do not use the plaster mold but send it to a foundry and have an aluminum or bronze copy made. To save yourself work later, make sure you carve out a pouring hole in the mold before sending it to the foundry. Even so, when the metal mold comes back from the foundry there is a lot of work to be done before it is ready to use. First you will have to file the face of the mold with a flat file so that it is level and smooth. Then file and grind the inside of the mold, using small triangular and pointed files or a small electric hand-grinding tool. Smooth out all the rough surfaces and corners of the mold and then finish the job with emery cloth, starting with a coarse grade and finally with a smooth grade. After the inside of the mold is fairly smooth, polish it with crocus cloth. The idea is to get the inside of the metal mold (which forms the squid) as smooth and polished as possible. Then, when you cast a metal squid it will come out smooth and shiny.

To get the mold ready for pouring you need a flat metal plate to use as a cover and you must file a slot in it for the hook. This metal plate can be about the same dimensions as the mold itself except that it doesn't have to be as thick. You can use a C-clamp to hold the plate against the mold when pouring the hot metal. To make a mold that is easier and quicker to use, get a flat, metal plate about one-half inch thick and the same length and width as the mold. Then tap the two sections of the mold to take screws so you can add handles and a hinge. Such a finished mold is shown in Fig. 107. However, it's more work to add the hinges and handles, so unless you plan to pour hundreds of metal squids, it is better to use one metal plate for all the molds you may have and clamp it in place each time.

Metal squids are basically made in two ways, one type having a stationary hook or fixed hook that is molded right into the body of the squid. The other type has a swinging hook that moves freely on an eye or escutcheon pin molded into the tail of the metal squid.

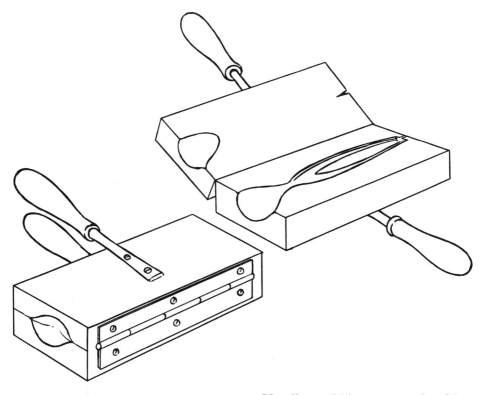

Figure 107.   *Handles and hinge on metal mold.*

These are shown in Fig. 108. Whichever type you make, allow for the hook or escutcheon pin or wire eye when cutting a slot or space in the mold or the cover so that it is held firmly in place while pouring. In other words, all the necessary parts must fit in place so that the mold can be closed tightly and the hook or pin or eye or nail stays in place while you are pouring.

After the metal squids have been poured they require some finishing. This can be done with a file first, then with steel wool to give the squid a smooth, shiny finish. The next step is to drill a hole at the front of the squid to which the fishing line is attached. This can be done with a hand drill but it is easier and faster with a drill press or electric drill. Then you get some brass eyelets or grommets and slip one into the hole. The eyelet can be set in place with a large punch or one of those special pliers used for the purpose. To complete the job, flatten or curl the protruding edge of the eyelet to hold it firmly in the hole. The eyelet will help strengthen the met-

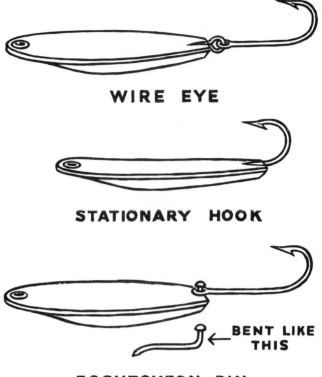

WIRE EYE

STATIONARY HOOK

ESCUTCHEON PIN

Three ways of attaching hooks to a metal squid.   *Figure 108.*

al squid at the eye and prevents the wire leader from cutting through the block tin, which is thin and narrow at this point.

To bring out the best action in the water, a metal squid is usually bent in a single or double bend as shown in Fig. 109. The thin, narrow metal squids are readily bent by hand, but the broader thicker ones have to be bent against a corner of a table or a vise.

The final step in making metal squids is to add feathers or hair at the tail or around the hook. You can, of course, use the plain squid to catch many fish. Or you can merely add a strip of pork rind to the hook. However, most anglers add white or yellow hackle feathers or bucktail hair to make the squid more attractive and effective. On a metal squid with a stationary hook you tie the feathers or bucktail around the tail end of the squid. Some anglers also add an additional swinging hook to the fixed one, as shown in Fig. 110. To do this you can open the eye of this second hook with a starting punch, slip it on the first hook, and then close it with pliers or a vise.

Figure 109.   *Two bends for bringing out action of metal squid.*

Figure. 110   *Adding second hook to metal squid.*

On a metal squid with a swinging hook you tie the feathers or hair around the hook itself, as shown in Fig. 111. This is best done on the hook alone before it is attached to the eye or pin of the metal squid.

If you do a lot of saltwater fishing, especially surf fishing, you'll lose many metal squids. So it pays to make up plenty of squids during the winter months or off-season so that you have plenty on hand when the fishing is good.

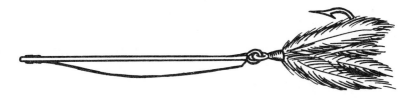

Feathers tied around hook.   **Figure 111.**

10

SALTWATER TUBE LURES

This chapter will cover the so-called tube lures made of plastic or surgical rubber tubing that have become very popular in recent years for saltwater fishing. Some tube lures such as the "bone" lure shown in Fig. 112 have been used for many years. In the old days these lures were actually made from the hollow, tubular animal bones such as those from cats, chickens, and turkeys. Today, with plastic tubes available in various diameters, thicknesses, lengths, and colors, very few natural bones are used.

Bone or plastic lure.   *Figure 112.*

To make the bone-type lure, buy some rigid white plastic tubing about ⅜ inch in diameter and cut it into lengths of about 3 or 4 inches long. Then tie a hook on a wire leader and slip the plastic tube down on the wire until it rests against the curve or bend of the hook. Although regular shank hooks can be used, a long-shank hook is usually preferred. Also a hook with a needle eye or small eye that can slip through the hole in the tube is better than a hook with a big ringed eye.

This bone lure can be used as it is, but many anglers prefer to dip a short section of the head in red paint or lacquer. Plastic tubing can also be obtained in other colors such as yellow, red, orange, blue, and green. Bone lures like this one are usually trolled for such fish as bluefish, mackerel, bonito, albacore, dolphin, and small tuna. When used for striped bass it's a good idea to add about two or three sandworms or bloodworms to the hook.

But the rigid bone lure is being replaced these days by the more flexible surgical rubber and plastic tube lures. These are now being made in various lengths and sizes, from tiny tube lures only one or two inches long, up to eighteen- or twenty-inch tube lures for big fish. The surgical tubing and plastic are available in various diameters and colors. You can buy them in some coastal fishing tackle stores or order them from some of the mail-order houses listed in the back of this book.

The tiny tube lures are easily made and can be used for many fish in fresh and salt water. You can obtain a few feet of the $\frac{3}{16}$-inch plastic tubing in white, yellow, pink, orange, red, blue, or brown and cut it into one-inch lengths. When cutting these small tube lures cut one end at an angle. Then get a small No. 4 or 6 long-shank hook and slip it into the hole in the tube (see Fig. 113). This tiny tube lure can be used in fresh water as it is or with some kind of bait to catch sunfish, white perch, yellow perch, and crappies.

Figure 113.

For saltwater fishing you can make up slightly larger tube lures in the same way using the same $\frac{3}{16}$-inch diameter tubing but cutting it into longer $1\frac{1}{2}$- or 2-inch lengths and running a larger No. 1 or 1/0 hook through the hole. Here the all clear or silver, white, yellow, pink, orange, and red tubing is best. When using these in salt water to catch such fish as mackerel, herring, small bluefish, pollock, and other fish, they are rigged about six or eight inches apart above a sinker or diamond jig. Usually anywhere from three to six lures are attached to short loops on the line (see Fig. 114).

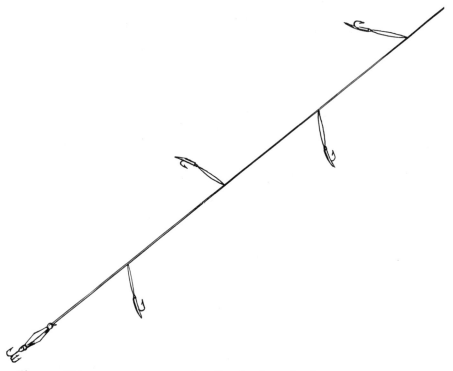

Figure 114.   Small, plastic tube lures rigged on line.

Then the whole series of tube lures are lowered from a bridge, pier, or boat into the water and are jigged up and down to attract and hook fish.

When anglers first discovered that surgical latex rubber will make good fishing lures, they started making short six- or eight-inch lures from this material. The natural light brown or amber-colored tubing was first used, but later they were able to obtain it in red, white, yellow, green, black, and purple, and started using these colors.

To make such a single hook tube lure, get some surgical tubing and cut off about a six- or seven-inch length. The tail should be sliced at an angle for about an inch and a half, so that the side of the tubing not removed forms a tapering tail. Then get a long-shanked hook such as the Pacific Bass in size 5/0 or 6/0 and tie a nylon monofilament leader to the hook eye. Then slide the rubber tube down the line toward the hook. The hook should be completely covered by the rubber tube allowing only the bend and

Figure 115.   *Rubber tube lure.*

point to protrude (see Fig. 115). Then bend the shank of the hook
to give the tube a slight curve so that it will have better action.
Because of this spinning action attach a good barrel or ball-bear-
ing swivel to the end of your leader. This lure is usually trolled
on the surface or underwater for such fish as bluefish, striped bass,
bonito, albacore, and pollock. If you want to cast it you have to add
a slip sinker or small, egg-shaped sinker on the leader ahead of
the rubber tube to provide weight (see Fig. 116).

Figure 116.   *Rubber tube lure weighted with a sinker.*

Another somewhat larger tube lure can be made from bright
surgical tubing such as white, yellow, pink, or fluorescent red. This
one is made by cutting a ten- or eleven-inch length of the tubing.
Then run a single-strand stainless steel wire through the tube, cutting it off on both ends so that enough wire remains to form eyes.
Now attach a treble hook to one end of the wire by means of a
haywire twist. On the other end run a slip sinker on the wire and
then push this sinker into the tubing so that it is partly buried.
Then form another eye with the remaining wire in front of the
sinker (see Fig. 117). This tube lure can be cast or trolled for
many saltwater species and is especially good for catching barracuda. But it can also be used for bluefish, snook, albacore, dolphin,
and king mackerel.

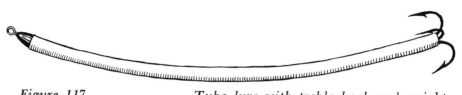

Figure 117.   *Tube lure with treble hook and weight.*

But if you want to catch big striped bass and bluefish, you can't beat the larger tube lures running up to eighteen or twenty inches and rigged with two big single hooks. To make this lure first cut the tube to the length you want the finished lure to be. A big heavy pair of sharp scissors is best for this and the tube at the tail should be sliced at an angle. Now take two No. 7/0 or 8/0 O'Shaughnessy hooks, open the eyes, and slip a barrel swivel on the eye of each hook, then close the eye. If you have trouble opening the eyes on these big hooks with pliers, use a starting punch to do this. And if the pliers fail to close the eye, use a vise to do this.

You can use braided wire, nylon coated wire, or monofilament line to rig the tube lure. Whichever is used it should test at least fifty or sixty pounds. Now take one of the hooks and attach about a two-foot length of the wire or mono line. Take the other hook and lay it against the front of the tube so that the center of the barrel swivel falls right at the opening in front of the tube. Now make a small slice in the tube where the hook begins to bend. This is where the front hook will protrude after it is pulled into the tube. The next step is to run the wire or line through the tube and out of the slice where the front hook will come out. Now pull the wire or line through the tube until the bend of the rear hook fits snugly in the hole and the tube begins to bend. Now attach the wire or line to the barrel swivel eye on the front or head hook. It is important that the distance between the rear hook and the front hook be just right so that the barrel swivel will be mostly buried inside the tube at the head. Now the final step is to pull the front hook shank and barrel swivel into the slot. To do this you need a wire needle or a piece of wire that is tied to the eye of the barrel swivel, and this is pulled into the slit and toward the head of the lure. (See Fig. 118 for some of the steps to follow in doing this.)

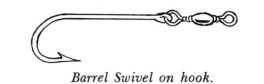

Barrel Swivel on hook.

Tube cut to size and rear hook attached to line.

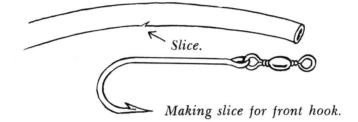

Making slice for front hook.

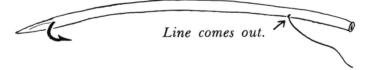

Rear hook pulled into tube.

Line tied to swivel on front hook.

Front hook pulled into slot and tube.

Figure 118.   *Steps in making two-hook surgical tube lure.*

The long, two-hook tube lures can be used as is for trolling on weighted or wire lines close to the bottom. You can also add various kinds of lead heads in front to provide weight. Or you can add different types of metal lips or action heads that are curved or bent to give the tube additional or varied action.

A good tube lure will have a certain spin resembling a corkscrew movement that appeals to fish. Some tubes work better than others even when made from the same type of tubing and the same size and length. That is why it's a good idea to make up many tubes in the same size and test these until you find the ones that are most effective.

To have a good action most of the tube lures must have a curve or two or three curves. You can form these curves by taking a cylindrical object such as a rolling pin, baseball bat, cardboard or plastic tube, or dowel rod and then wrapping the tube around it to form the curves (see Fig. 119).

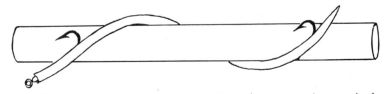

Figure 119.   *Forming curve in surgical tube.*

It will take a lot of tinkering and experimenting until you learn how to turn out tube lures that work well and catch fish. But it is difficult to turn out uniform tube lures, since each section of rubber takes its own peculiar curvature and sets that way. So tube lures will always vary in action to a certain extent. Some will turn out to be "fish killers" while others will be duds and poor fish catchers. But the fact that you can make your own tube lures cheaply works in your favor. You can afford to discard the "lemons" and keep the best lures. But if you have to buy the tube lures ready made at a high price, you are stuck with them and hate to throw them away.

11

EEL AND EELSKIN LURES

Eel and eelskin lures are not strictly artificial lures but are included in this book because they are very effective lures in saltwater fishing and many anglers would like to know how to rig and make them. Besides, although made from the natural eel, they are used like artificial lures—being cast or trolled and given action in the water. Also many of these lures make use of metal parts besides the eel itself. Eel and eelskin lures are used mostly in salt water to catch such fish as striped bass, bluefish, snook, and marlin.

The most difficult part about making eel and eelskin lures will often be obtaining the eels themselves. The eel usually used is the so-called common eel found from Labrador to Brazil along the Atlantic Coast. The female eels often reach several pounds in weight and live in freshwater rivers, streams, and lakes. The males are much smaller and live in saltwater bays, sounds, and tidal creeks. These are the ones usually used for bait.

Live eels are caught with eel pots, baited with dead fish, small baitfish, crushed clams, or crabs. These pots, which are similar to minnow traps, are wire cages with funnel entrances on both ends. The eels enter through the funnel holes, but once inside have trouble finding their way out. Live or frozen eels can also be purchased from many fish markets, bait dealers, and fishing-tackle stores. The size of the eel will depend on the fishing tackle you use and the fish you want to catch. Small eels from eight to twelve inches long are best with light tackle such as spinning outfits for small or medium-sized fish. The larger eels from twelve to twenty inches are used with heavier surf outfits and for trolling offshore for big fish.

To rig an eel you need a long needle such as an upholsterer's needle. It should be anywhere from twelve to fourteen inches long. You can make your own needle, using a brass or copper or stainless-steel rod about one-eighth inch in diameter. One end should be filed to a sharp point while the other end has an eye or a slot to which a line can be tied. You also need some 6/0, 7/0, 8/0, or 9/0 hooks, again depending on the size of the eel used and the fish sought. The larger the eel, the larger the hooks required. Light tackle and lines and small fish require smaller hooks than heavier fishing tackle and big fish. The O'Shaughnessy pattern of hook is usually used for rigging eels, but some anglers prefer the Siwash or salmon pattern, and still others use Eagle Claw hooks. Whichever type of hook you use, it should have a ringed eye. Finally you need some linen or braided nylon fishing line testing forty-five to sixty pounds. If bluefish are sought, some anglers rig their eels with wire, but fishing line gives you a more flexible eel with better action and is strong enough for striped bass, which is the fish usually sought with rigged eels.

There are many ways to rig an eel, but the method described here is one of the most popular and produces a rigged eel that stands up well. The first step is to tie about eighteen inches of the heavy line to the eye of the needle, and tie one of the hooks to the other end (see Fig. 120). Next, insert the needle into the underside of the eel at the vent (the small opening about four or five inches from the end of the eel's tail) and push the needle through the eel inside of the body until it emerges from the mouth. Then pull the needle until the line also comes out of the eel's mouth (see Fig. 121). The hook shank is then buried inside the eel by pulling on the line. Now, double back the needle and push the point into the eel's mouth and force it out at the neck about two inches from the nose. Pull the needle through the hole the needle has made (see Fig. 122) and untie the line from the needle. This leaves a loop of line protruding from the mouth and the end of the line emerging from the eel's neck. Tie another hook to the end of this line and pull on the loop to bring the hook shank inside the eel (see Fig. 123).

The final step is to provide a bridle. Take about four or five inches of thin, flexible brass wire and run one end into the eel's mouth and out the gill opening on one side. Pull more wire out of this opening, run it over the top of the eel's head, push the end through the gill opening on the opposite side of the head, force it out through the eel's mouth, and then tie the two ends of wire protruding from the eel's mouth around the loop of line several times (see Fig. 124). You can also use fishing line instead of the wire to make a bridle.

The eel can be used as is with the fishing line being tied to

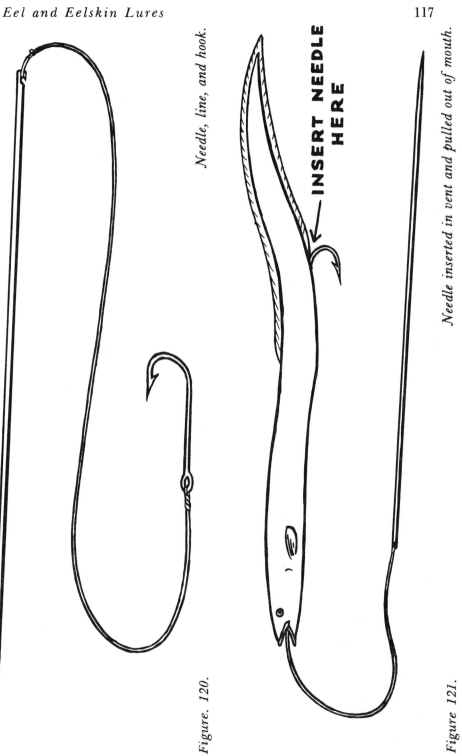

Needle, line, and hook.

INSERT NEEDLE HERE

Needle inserted in vent and pulled out of mouth.

Figure. 120.

Figure 121.

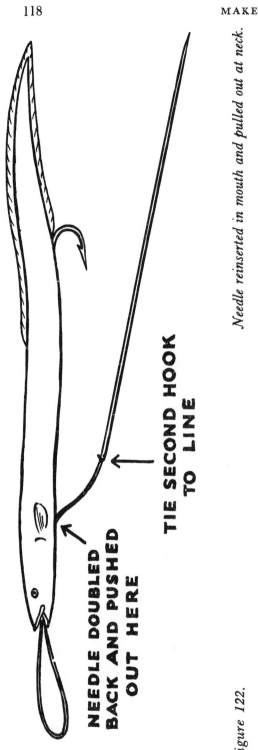

**NEEDLE DOUBLED
BACK AND PUSHED
OUT HERE**

**TIE SECOND HOOK
TO LINE**

Needle reinserted in mouth and pulled out at neck.

Figure 122.

Finished rigged eel with two hooks.

Figure 123.

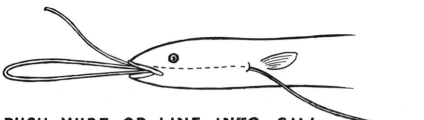

PUSH WIRE OR LINE INTO GILL
AND OUT OF MOUTH

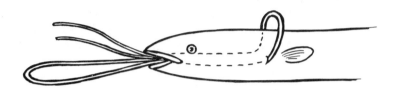

TAKE OTHER END OF WIRE AND PUSH
THROUGH GILL OPENING ON OPPOSITE SIDE
AND OUT OF MOUTH

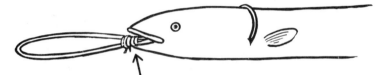

TIE ENDS OF WIRE AROUND LOOP OF
LINE AT EEL'S MOUTH

Figure 124.   *Tying a bridle on a rigged eel's head.*

the loop. Or you can attach a small barrel swivel to this loop, since the eel has a tendency to spin at times when reeled fast or in a current. Some anglers also tie some line around the body of the eel where the hook emerges to reinforce it. You can also tie some line around the eel's mouth to close it tightly so no water can enter.

Some anglers also use a brass chain, such as the type used for windows, to rig an eel. The chain is very strong and is preferred when there are bluefish around. These sharp-toothed fish will bite through ordinary line, but the chain holds them. And, of course, chain doesn't rot or weaken like line or cord.

A rigged eel works fairly well with nothing else attached, but many saltwater fishermen also rig them with various gadgets, action heads, and weights, which give the eels more movement and weight for casting. One way to do this is to attach a small metal squid at the head of the eel, as shown in Fig. 125. You need a small, wide, metal squid that has an eye in the middle of the body to which the line leading to the hooks is attached. Or you can drill two holes in the metal squid, tie the line through them, and rig your eel in the same manner as described above. To attach the metal squid, force the hook through the neck of the eel and out on top, then tie the line protruding from the eel's mouth to the eye on top of the squid or the two holes—whichever the metal squid has. Finally, tie several turns of thin fishing line around the eel's head, lashing it to the metal squid.

Eel rigged with small metal squid.   *Figure 125*

The eel-rigging methods described above are used for inshore fishing for striped bass and bluefish. For offshore trolling for such fish as marlin and school tuna you need a stronger eel, and here you can use stainless-steel wire and large 7/0 or 8/0 hooks. One hook is used at the head, and this is inserted into the eel's mouth and out at the neck so that the eye of the hook rests inside the eel's mouth. Then run the wire through the eel's nose, into the eye of the hook, and form a loop by twisting the wire as shown in chapter 14. (See Fig. 126 for an eel rigged in this manner.)

An old-time method of adding weight to an eel is to make an eel bob, as shown in Fig. 127. Here you cut off the eel's head, pull the skin back for about two inches, and cut out the meat. Then you rig the eel with one or two hooks in the regular way and insert a cylindrical lead weight into the skin. The lead weight should have a hole through the middle so that the line or chain used in

Wire runs through jaws of eel and through eye of hook.
Figure 126.   *Rigging eel for offshore trolling.*

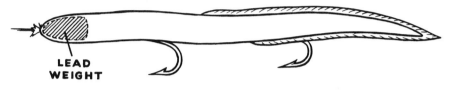

Eel bob.   Figure 127.

rigging can be run into it and out in front. After this is done, the skin of the eel is tied ahead of the lead weight, concealing it and keeping it in place. Such an eel bob can be made any length using most of the eel or just the tail section.

Another way to rig an eel and provide action and weight at the same time is to add a metal wobble plate at the head, as shown in Fig. 128. The metal plate can be made from copper tubing or pipe, the diameter depending on the weight you want and the size of the eel. A copper pipe about five-eighths inch in diameter is a good all-around size to use. You cut off about three inches of this pipe, then flatten half that length in a vise, bend it in the middle, and curve

Eel rigged with wobble plate.   Figure 128.

the upper end, as shown in Fig. 129. Drill one hole near the end of the flattened section for the fishing line or leader and another hole where the pipe is round to hold the hook. Then the eel is rigged in the usual manner with the head of the eel being inserted into the hole of the wobble plate together with the hook eye inside the eel's mouth. A cotter pin or small bolt is then run through the hole in the pipe, through the eel's head and through the eye of the hook. You can also tie the line used to rig the eel to the cotter pin or bolt. You'll find it easier if you first pierce the eel's head with an ice pick or awl before you try to insert the pin or bolt through it. To further reinforce the eel, tie cord around the eel's neck and lash it to the shank of the hook.

BOLT AND NUT

Pipe bent to form a wobble plate.   *Figure 129.*

Instead of using the entire eel, many saltwater anglers use just the skin from the eel to make effective lures. You can catch the eels and skin them yourself or you can buy the skins already packed in jars. The simplest type of eelskin rig is made from a copper or brass tube or pipe (see Fig. 130). The diameter of the tube or pipe will depend on the size and length of the eelskin you use. The small-diameter tubes are best for shorter skins from small eels,

Figure 130.   *Eelskin rig made from a pipe section.*

while the larger ones are used for the longer, wider eelskins. Cut off about 1½ inches of the pipe and drill holes at both ends. If you use a shorter length of pipe you need only one hole in the middle. Now with a triangular file, make a groove all around the pipe at one end. Now get some brass chain and attach two hooks to this chain. The length of the chain and the distance between the two hooks will depend on the length of the eelskin you use. Now get a couple of sets of bolts and nuts. The bolts should be long enough and thin enough to fit through the holes drilled in the copper pipe. Start one of the bolts through the front end of the pipe, slip a barrel swivel on the bolt inside the copper pipe, and run the bolt through the other hole (see Fig. 130). Then run the other bolt through the holes on the other end of the pipe. But before you do this slip the last link of the chain on the bolt inside the pipe. The final step is to slip the eelskin over the two hooks, piercing the skin and allowing the points and barbs to protrude. Then tie the eelskin to the copper pipe with fishing line around the groove, making certain that the line holds the skin tightly.

Another type of eelskin rig uses a weighted lead head similar to the heads used in making jigs (see Fig. 131). You can mold such

Eelskin lure.   *Figure 131.*

a head in the same way as described in chapter 7, except that when casting a weighted head you attach another hook to the eye of the first one, using stainless-steel wire. The wire is wound through the eye of the first hook and a loop extends beyond it for four or five inches (see Fig. 132). You don't have to add the second hook be-

Hook prepared with wire loop, ready for the eelskin lure mold. Figure 132.

fore pouring the metal head—all you need is the wire loop to which the hook can be added later. After the head of the lure is molded, solder a ring around it so that the eelskin can be tied around it. Such rings can be made easily from brass or copper pipe or tubing by cutting off sections at one-fourth-inch intervals. A small pipe cutter can be used to do this quickly. Then file a groove around the ring so that the eelskin can be tied to it. (See Fig. 133 showing such a ring soldered in place on the head of the lure.)

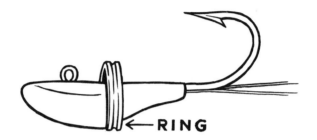

Ring soldered to the head of an eelskin lure.   *Figure 134.*

You can also use similar rings to make an eelskin squid as shown in Fig. 134. To make such a lure use almost any metal squid with a swinging-type hook. Smaller metal squids will, of course, require smaller rings than larger squids. The ring is slipped over the metal squid and is sweated on with a soldering iron held against the ring. You can drop some solder where the ring lies against the metal squid. To finish the lure, slip an eelskin over the hook and the tail end of the squid and tie the skin around the ring with fishing line or thread. You just puncture the eelskin so that the hook protrudes as shown in the illustration.

Eelskins are also used over plugs to give them a more natural look. Here you have to remove all the hooks, slip the eelskin on,

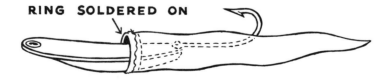

Eelskin attached to a metal squid.   *Figure 133.*

then replace the hooks. The eelskin is tied in front and at the rear with fishing line to make sure it stays in place. The skin should be long enough so that three inches or so of the tail extends beyond the plug to flutter in the water when reeled or trolled.

Lures made with eels will last a long time if you keep them frozen or in a container filled with heavy brine. Eelskins will keep a long time in such salt brine in an air-tight glass jar or similar container. However, many anglers prefer to rig their eelskins and eels fresh before each fishing trip. A freshly killed eel is tough and will take more abuse and stand up longer. Eels that have been kept preserved for any length of time tend to soften and fall apart.

Rigging natural eels or eelskin lures is often a messy job and quite a bit of trouble. But many anglers feel that they are still superior to artificial or plastic eels because, besides looking like the real thing, they also have a smell or scent that helps to attract fish such as striped bass.

12

OTHER LURES

There are many other kinds of lures that can be made easily and quickly at little cost with a wide variety of materials. It is surprising how many commercially made items used for other purposes can also be converted or adapted for fishing lures. Like the common plastic straw used to sip ice-cream sodas or pop—you can buy these in boxes in different colors at almost any grocery, supermarket, or notions store.

To make a small lure from these plastic straws all you have to do is cut them into one-inch or slightly longer lengths. Cut them straight on one end and diagonally at the other end. Then get a No. 4 or No. 6 long-shank hook and slip the straw over the shank. You can use these lures singly with or without a plastic float. Or you can rig them in series and tie a weight on the end of your line or a small, diamond jig and then add four or five of the straw lures above this weight. The straw lures can be used in fresh water for panfish and in salt water for snapper blues, mackerel, and herring.

Other lures for herring shad, small bluefish, and similar fish can be made quickly with a hook and some tin or aluminum foil, tinsel, or cellophane. Take a small hook, such as a No. 2 or 4, in regular shank or long shank, depending on how big you want the lure to be, and wrap the foil or cellophane around it, and then tie the ends with red nylon or other thread. Such a lure is shown in Fig. 135. If you want you can also add a few feathers or hair to the tail of the lure.

Another lure made by saltwater anglers who fish for herring or mackerel or shad is shown in Fig. 136. It can be made from any shiny metal such as nickel, chrome-plated brass, or stainless steel.

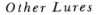

Tin foil wrapped on a hook. *Figure 135.*

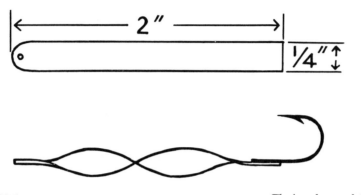

Figure 136. *Twisted metal lure.*

This lure should be made small for herring and other small fish, say about two inches long and one-fourth inch wide. The thickness or gauge of the metal used will depend on the weight you want. Metal about .04 inch thick is good for the size of the lure suggested here. After the lure is cut out it is polished or buffed and then twisted as shown in the drawing. Then a hole should be drilled on one end for the fishing line. If you use a single hook you can either solder it or rivet it to the metal body. If you use a small treble hook, drill a larger hole on the end and add a split ring and then attach the hook to this. This lure is kind of light for casting but can be jigged up and down from a pier, dock, boat, or other spot where there is fairly deep water and where mackerel or herring are present. It can also be used in saltwater for snapper blues, hickory shad, and other small fish. And you can also try it in fresh water jigging and ice fishing for yellow perch, white perch, walleyes, and pickerel.

Another excellent jigging lure can be made quickly and easily by obtaining solid cylindrical or even hexagonal metal bars in various diameters and cutting them into different lengths. Brass or copper bars are somewhat expensive but you can use chrome-plated steel bars instead. Then cut the bars into the length and weight lure you want. The bars should be cut at an angle or slant at both ends. Then drill a hole on each end and add split rings. To complete the lure you add a heavy treble hook on one end and it is ready for jigging (see Fig. 137). It can be used in salt water to catch bluefish, mackerel, cod, pollock, lingcod, rockfish, grouper, and snappers. You can also use it in fresh water when deep-jigging for lake trout.

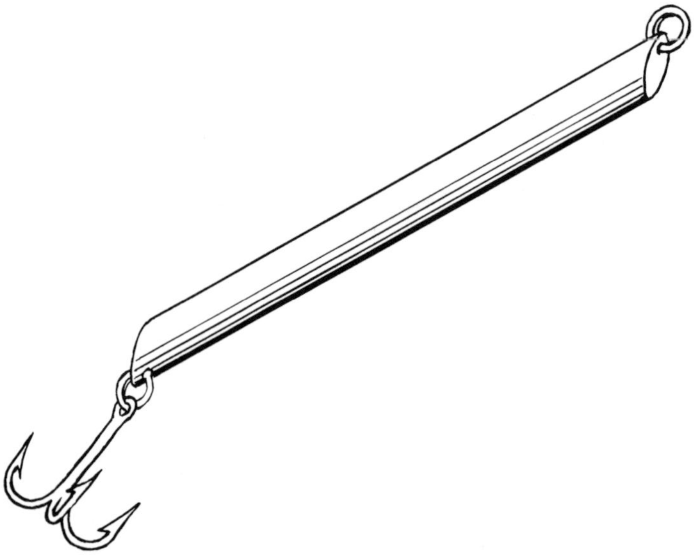

Figure 137.   *Solid metal rod jigging lure.*

An ordinary clothespin can be used to make a wide variety of fresh and saltwater fishing lures. You can make tiny bass bugs or spin bugs by just using the front part of the clothespin and cutting off the legs. Or you can take the entire clothespin, add a couple of hooks, and make a surface popping plug out of it by using it as it is or cutting a slant in front or a notch at the head.

Or you can drill a hole through the head of the clothespin, then run a wire leader through the hole, attach a big single hook at the tail, and pull it through so that the hook lies in the space between the legs. Or if you want to use a feather hook or bucktail hook or plastic skirt you can make the hook rest against the slot or end of the clothespin. This lure can be used for trolling in salt water.

To make a heavier or more solid clothespin lure you can fill in the empty space between the legs with plastic wood or wood filler or just insert a strip of wood between the legs and glue it in place. You can also tie the legs together with line and fill the remaining space between the legs with plastic wood or glue.

Fig. 138 shows some clothespin lures you can make, but the variations you can make from this ordinary household item are endless. You can spray or paint the body of the lure any color you want to make it more attractive to fish.

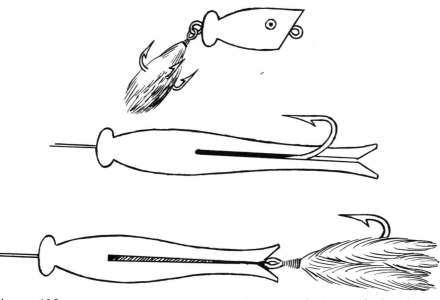

Figure 138.   *Lures made from clothespin.*

In recent years the so-called umbrella lures have made a big hit with the fish and fishermen especially along the Atlantic coast, where they are used for striped bass, bluefish, pollock, and other fish. These are multiple-lure rigs that have several small tube lures attached to wire arms and look like a small school of baitfish swimming through the water.

A simple umbrella lure can be made with a lead weight and two lengths of wire. You can use almost any fairly strong, hard wire in the heavier gauges to form the arms, but stainless steel in the heavier thicknesses is best since it has great strength yet a spring-like flexibility that gives the lures better action.

Then you get a lead head or weight with a hole through it and drill two more holes in the sides and force the wire arms through them so that they form a cross. The wire arms should extend about eight inches beyond the lead head. Then you form an eye at the center of the arm and another one on each end. Then run a short length of wire through the head of the lead weight and attach a barrel swivel on each side, one for the fishing line and the lower one to hold the center tube lure. This umbrella will hold nine tube lures, five of which will have hooks, while the smaller ones will be teasers without hooks. The four outside tube lures can be rigged on short monofilament leaders to suspend them from the arms (see Fig. 139).

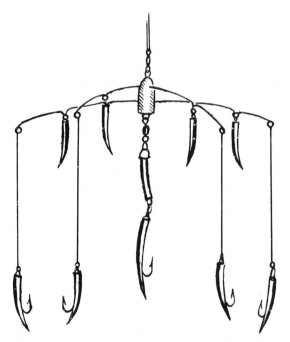

Figure 139.   *Finished umbrella rig.*

The plastic tube lures used with the umbrella rig are similar to those described in chapter 10 dealing with tube lures. They will vary in the diameter and length of the tube and the size of the hook according to the fish you are seeking. For small fish you can use the smaller, thinner tubes, while for the larger fish you use the longer, bigger tubes and stronger hooks. The tubes can be different colors or all the same color with white, silver, yellow, pink, orange, red, and black usually used. The umbrella rig is trolled deep on wire line for best results.

You can also make a wide variety of lures using those colorful plastic or rubber skirts that come in different lengths and colors. Take the jig heads you made and just slip one of these skirts over the hook and onto the jig and wrap some thread around it to hold it in place. The same thing can be done with a metal squid. Add a fluorescent pink, orange, or red plastic or rubber tail to the metal squid, and it will often attract more fish than other materials. You can also take these skirts and rig them in tandem, with two or three of them one behind the other. This will look like a squid when trolled through the water and will appeal to saltwater fish that feed on these jet-propelled baits (see Fig. 140).

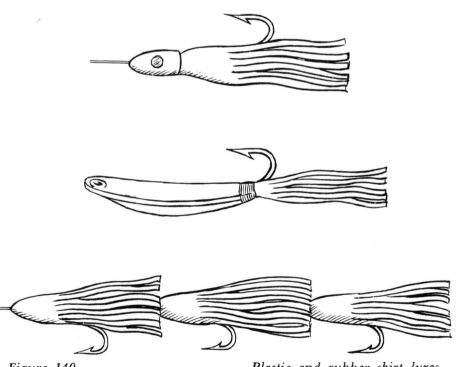

Figure 140.   *Plastic and rubber skirt lures.*

One problem often encountered in both fresh and saltwater fishing is how to cast a tiny lure such as a small panfish bug, a tiny spoon or spinner, or a light jig with heavy fishing tackle. Some of these lures may weigh only a fraction of an ounce and are too light to cast with spinning, bait-casting, or surf rods. To get around this problem and at the same time create a rig that attracts fish, anglers have made up "splasher" combination rigs.

A splasher rig consists of a cylindrical section of wood that has an eye on each end. The fishing line is tied to one eye, and a nylon monofilament leader anywhere from a foot to two feet long is tied to the other eye. The length of this leader and the thickness of the wood splasher will depend on the tackle you are using. Short leaders and small splashers are used with freshwater tackle and longer leaders and bigger splashers are used with saltwater rods.

On the end of the leader you tie on a small panfish bug or bass bug for freshwater fishing. Or tie on a small spoon or tiny jig for fresh or saltwater fishing. The idea here is to use the block of wood or splasher as a weight for casting, with the small lure trailing behind. The wood section floats and when jerked or trolled creates a commotion or splash that attracts fish.

The cylindrical section of wood can be made from any round wood, such as a dowel, a broomstick, or tool handle. Choose the smaller diameters and cut them to shorter lengths for freshwater and light tackle. Pick the larger diameters and cut them longer for saltwater use.

For the smaller freshwater splashers you can use two screw eyes, one on each end, for tying on the fishing line and leader. But for the larger splashers used in saltwater fishing the through-wire construction with eyes formed at each end is stronger. This, of course, requires drilling a hole through the center of the splasher for the wire. You can use the splasher rig as is, but many anglers like to paint the wood white, yellow, silver, or any other light color for better visibility in the water. Fig. 141 shows a completed splasher rig and the way it is attached ahead of a lure.

2 FOOT NYLON LEADER

LURE

Figure 141.   Wood splasher rig.

13

SINKERS

Fishing sinkers can't be called "lures," but since they are widely used and many anglers mold their own, they are included in this book. Also, making sinkers is simliar in many ways to molding metal squids or jigs. By the nature of their use, sinkers are lost even more often than most fishing lures, so it really pays to make your own.

There are many types, such as the ball or round, bell or dipsey, bank, oval, flat, rectangular, pencil, and pyramid. These are illustrated in Fig. 142 and will give you an idea of the different types of sinkers used in fresh and saltwater fishing.

You don't need much equipment to make sinkers. A gas or electric stove is required to melt the lead or other metal and a ladle to hold and pour the molten lead. For making sinkers, especially the heavier, saltwater types, a big ladle is best. You also need lead, which is usually used to make sinkers. Scrap lead can usually be obtained from a junk dealer. Alloys of lead and other metals such as type metal can also be used to make sinkers although you usually get best results with pure lead. Finally you need a mold of some sort.

One of the easiest and quickest sinkers to make is the flat, oval type used in freshwater fishing or light-tackle saltwater angling. For a mold, use either an old teaspoon or tablespoon, depending on how big and heavy you want the sinker to be. Then melt the lead and pour it into the spoon (see Fig. 143). You can control the size and weight of the sinker by regulating the amount of lead you pour. If the sinker tends to stick to the spoon after pouring, just wipe the spoon with an oily rag before pouring the next one. After the sinkers are poured and cool, you drill or punch a hole

RECTANGULAR   BALL   DIPSEY   BANK

OVAL

DIAMOND   PENCIL   PYRAMID

Figure 142.   *Types of sinkers.*

← PUNCH OUT HOLE
WITH NAIL

Figure 143.   *Using a spoon to make a sinker.*

in one end for the fishing line and the sinker is completed. These flat sinkers hold bottom very well and do not roll in the current or tide.

Another simple and quick way to make sinkers is with a potato mold. Just take a large potato, cut it in half, and then carve out a cavity for the type of sinker you want. Since this is a one-piece mold where you use only one half of the potato, you are naturally limited to the type of sinkers you can make. You can make rectangular, dipsey or bell, pyramid and cylindrical, or pencil-type sinkers. Although you can pour some of these sinkers and then drill eyes in the lead later on, you can also cut a slot in the bottom of the cavity and put a wire eye into it. Then pour the hot lead into the cavity and when it cools pull out the finished sinker. Such a potato mold with the position of the wire eye is shown in Fig. 144. When you pour the first sinkers you'll find that the moist potato will sputter and sizzle. But after you pour two or three sinkers it will dry out and then you'll have no more difficulty in this regard. Naturally, the potato mold doesn't last very long, and after a while it dries up and shrivels too much to be of any use. However, a potato mold is inexpensive and so simple that you can make another one in a matter of minutes.

Another inexpensive and simple way you can make a mold is by using a chunk of hard wood and drilling and carving out a sinker cavity. Here too, the mold is one piece and you are limited to

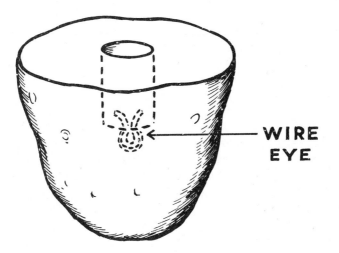

Potato mold.   *Figure 144.*

the types of sinkers made with the potato mold. You can make a good dipsey or bell sinker mold from a wood block by drilling a cavity on one end with different size drills. First start with a large-size drill and drill only a short distance into the wood. Then use a slightly smaller drill and go a bit deeper, then a still smaller one to reach the full depth you want, after which you can use a knife and gouge to smoothen out the inside and get rid of the ridges. Wood-carving tools are also good for this work. Cut a small slot in the far end of the cavity to take a wire eye and the mold is ready to use. Such a mold is shown in Fig. 145. It will last quite a while before the hot metal burns it out too much for use.

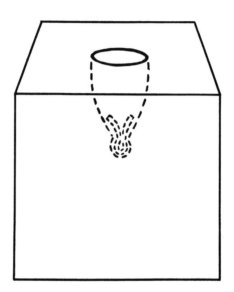

Wooden sinker mold.   *Figure 146.*

If you have a drill press or an electric drill and other metal-working tools you can make such a one-piece mold from a piece of metal. Brass, copper, bronze, and aluminum are easiest to drill and cut, but you can also use iron and drill out a sinker cavity similar to the wooden mold described above. Once made, such a mold will last forever and will make thousands of sinkers.

When making molds for the other types of sinkers such as the ball or bank you have to make a two-piece mold similar to the types made for jigs described in chapter 7. These can be made from plaster of Paris or water putty or dental cement if you want temporary, inexpensive molds. In making such a two-piece mold, you can have two cavities and pour two sinkers at a time instead of one (see Fig. 146). So when you get a cardboard box or make a wooden frame for such a mold make sure it is big enough to take the two cavities.

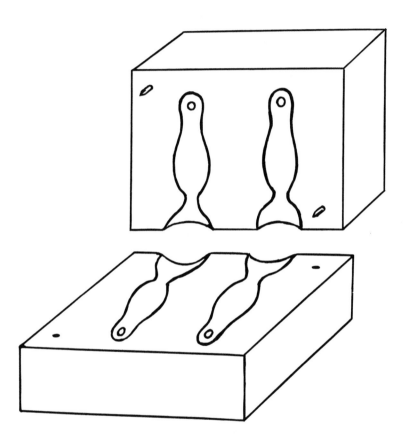

Figure 145.   *Sinker mold with two cavities.*

As noted, the procedures in making a plaster of Paris or water putty mold are similar to those described earlier in the chapter on making jigs. However, instead of using the actual sinker for a pattern, you should carve such a sinker pattern from soft wood, wax, or soap or form it from clay. The lead sinker itself cannot be used because it is too heavy and will sink into the wet plaster all the

way instead of only halfway. So when making such a mold, push
the sinker pattern into the wet plaster halfway and then wait until the plaster sets and hardens. Then grease or oil the top of this
plaster and the pattern showing and pour the other half of the
mold.

You can also make two-piece plaster of Paris molds to pour various types of trolling weights as shown in Fig. 147. These trolling

Two types of trolling weights.   *Figure 147.*

weights are usually cylindrical or keel shaped and have eyes on
each end to which the fishing line or leaders are attached. When
making a two-piece mold to pour such trolling weights you must
cut out grooves on both ends of the cavity to take such wire eyes
or barrel swivels on each end. Such a mold for making trolling
sinkers and weights is shown in Fig. 148.

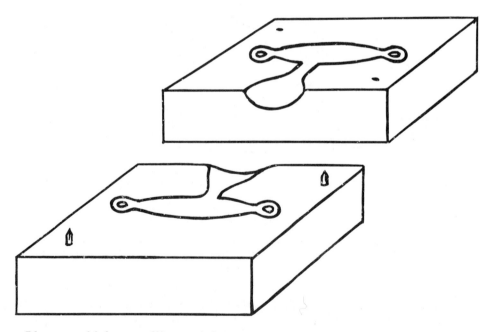

Plaster mold for a trolling weight.   *Figure 148.*

The potato, wood, and plaster molds described above will last long enough to make anywhere from a dozen to two or three dozen sinkers. If you want a permanent mold that will last indefinitely, make a plaster mold of the type you want and take it to foundry and have a bronze or aluminum mold made. This is best if you have a special design or type or size you want and can't find a ready-made mold.

But you can buy ready-made molds for the regular or standard types of sinkers in almost any fishing-tackle store. You can also order them by mail from some of the supply houses listed in the back of this book. Such permanent molds are inexpensive and will last a long time.

When using metal sinker molds a few words of advice are in order. Make sure your mold is warm and dry, and heat the lead well above the melting point before pouring it into the mold. Otherwise, the molten metal will solidify and form imperfect sinkers before it has a chance to reach all parts of the mold. After a while you'll be able to tell what the best pouring temperature is by watching the color of the molten metal. When pouring sinkers and weights, remember that it's a good idea to scoop the scum and dirt off the top of the molten lead at regular intervals so that it pours with no trouble.

14

LEADERS AND CONNECTIONS

Leaders and connections such as snaps and swivels also cannot be considered "lures," but they are used with lures and are vital when it comes to catching fish. Most fresh and saltwater anglers tie or make their own leaders. In fact, with increased fishing pressure and more fishermen on the lakes, rivers, and oceans, fish are more wary and harder to catch. To hook many of these fish you must use a leader that is not too noticeable between the fishing line and the lure, and after the fish is hooked your leader must hold him without being cut or broken during the fight. Finally, leaders are usually heavier and stronger than the main line in order to absorb shocks of casting and wear and tear. They are also stronger than the main fishing line in order to stand the constant rubbing and friction against the guides on the rod and the sand, rocks, and other obstructions in the water.

With the development of nylon by DuPont a major advance was made in fishing lines and leaders. Nylon monofilament is strong and smooth, resists wear and tear, is waterproof, and is almost invisible. You can buy coils of nylon monofilament in various strengths from about a pound or less up to 150 pounds or more. You'll find that for most freshwater spinning you'll need nylon leaders testing six, eight, ten, or twelve pounds. When you are after larger fish, such as lake trout, coho salmon and pike, or muskellunge, you may need leaders up to thirty pounds or so. It also depends on the fishing line you are using. The leader should be a few pounds heavier than the main fishing line. For saltwater fishing, nylon monofilament leaders testing from eight or ten pounds up to twenty or thirty pounds are usually used. Surf anglers sometimes use thirty to sixty-pound test leaders and big-game anglers may resort to leaders up to 150 to 200 pounds. But in this book we are mainly concerned with the leaders used with the lures described in previous chapters used for fish weighing from a pound up to fifty or sixty pounds or so.

The length of the nylon monofilament leader will depend on the tackle you use. Generally, it should be long enough so that when you reel in most of your line on a spinning reel and are ready to cast again, there will be a few turns of the leader on your reel. In other words, the leader should run from the reel to the rod tip and beyond to the lure. With bait-casting outfits and conventional surf rods the leader can be up to the reel, but no turns of the leader would be on the reel itself. The reason is that spinning lines are thin and the knots joining the leader with the main fishing line are small. But with thicker leaders and fishing lines a knot on your reel may hamper your casting by getting caught by the line.

When you cast, most of the shock will be absorbed by the stronger leader instead of the weaker fishing line. So, most such leaders will run from five or six feet up to eighteen or twenty feet for big surf outfits. Of course, for light-tackle trolling the leaders can be shorter, and when you use a wire or stainless steel leader for casting it can be only a few inches long.

To make nylon monofilament leaders you must know how to tie good, strong knots. A knot is the weakest link in your line or leader. Even a perfectly tied knot tends to weaken a line or leader, but a wrong or carelessly tied knot can weaken your line or leader by as much as fifty percent or more. A good knot properly tied weakens the line by ten or twenty percent or so.

Sailors, riggers, and fishermen use many different kinds of knots. For most fishing needs and for tying leaders, however, only a few basic knots are required, and these are shown in Fig. 149. Nylon knots have a tendency to slip if not properly tied, so care must be taken when tightening the knot. After the knot is formed it should be pulled up slowly, and then pulled hard to tighten it. After the knot is tied, do not clip the end off too short on most knots. For certain knots it is also a good idea to burn this end with a match or cigarette lighter so that the nylon fuses into a tiny ball.

Here's how to tie the four basic knots shown in Fig. 149. The blood knot (A), also called the barrel knot, is used to join lines or leaders. To tie it, first lap the ends of the line or leader. Then twist one end around the line to make at least five turns. Next place the end between the strands and hold them together between

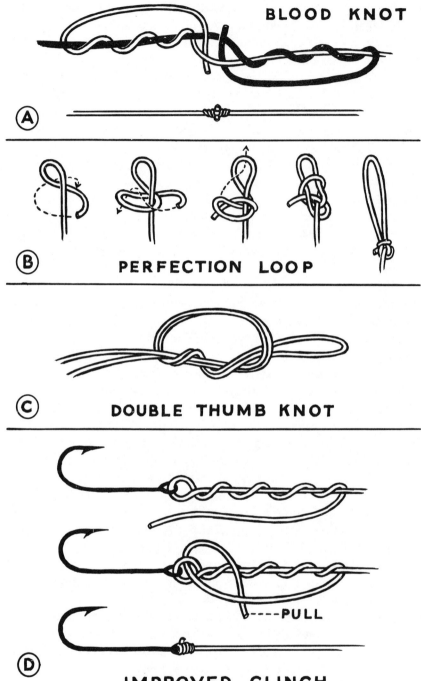

BLOOD KNOT

(A)

PERFECTION LOOP

(B)

DOUBLE THUMB KNOT

(C)

----PULL

IMPROVED CLINCH

(D)

Basic leader knots.   *Figure 149.*

your thumb and forefinger. Now wind the other end around the line for the same number of turns, in the opposite direction, and place it between the strands. Finally, pull on the two ends to draw the turns closer together. When they bunch up, pull tight and hard on the ends, making the knot as small as possible. Then clip off the ends as close to the knot as possible.

The perfection loop knot (B) is for tying a loop on the end of your line or leader. Here you take one looping turn around the nylon and hold the lines together between your thumb and forefinger. Then take a second looping turn around the crossing. Next, take the big loop formed by this second turn, pass it through the loop on top, and pull on this big loop until the knot jams. Then clip off the end.

The double thumb knot (C) is another knot that can be used to tie a loop on the end of a line or leader. Here you merely double your leader for a few inches to form a long, narrow loop and then tie a simple overhand knot twice, as shown.

The improved clinch knot (D) is used for tying a leader to the hook, snap, or lure. To tie it, run about three or four inches of the end of the leader through the eye, then double it back and twist it around the leader for at least five turns. Next, put the end through the opening next to the eye, and, for added security, run the end through the big loop formed by the nylon. To tighten, pull on the end and slide the turns toward the eye. To finish, clip off the end.

In order to save fishing time it pays to make up the nylon leaders in advance, tying a loop on one end and attaching a swivel and snap on the other end. Then coil the leader and put it into a separate paper, cellophane, or glassine envelope. It's also a good idea to mark the length and strength of the leader on the envelope somewhere so that you don't get confused later on.

When fishing in fresh water for pike and muskies and for many saltwater fish you need a wire leader ahead of the lure to prevent these fish from biting through the nylon leader. When surf fishing it's a good idea to attach a short wire leader to all your lures, such as metal squids and plugs (see Fig. 150). Then tie a snap-swivel

Figure 150.   *Short wire leader on a lure.*

on your line for changing the lures. Such a short wire leader can run anywhere from six to twelve inches in length.

Two kinds of metal leaders are usually used for fishing: the single strand wire and cable wire. The single strand is made from stainless-steel wire and is best for most fishing. It is widely used for saltwater leaders, and you can buy it by the coil in most fishing tackle stores.

Stainless-steel wire comes in various diameters and strengths, from No. 2, which tests only 27 pounds, on up to No. 18, which tests about 325 pounds. The lower numbers are used for freshwater fishing and light saltwater angling—the higher numbers are used for surf fishing and big saltwater fish.

To make metal leaders from stainless-steel wire you'll need diagonal cutting pliers, flat-nose pliers, and round-nosed pliers. For thinner wire you can use the smaller jeweler's round-nosed pliers. For the heavier leaders the bigger round-nosed pliers are better.

The whole secret in making wire leaders is learning how to form and twist the eyes on the ends properly. It's surprising how few fresh or saltwater anglers know how to make a neat, secure eye on a wire leader. Most of the wire leaders are crudely formed and often insecure or slide and tighten. Many surf anglers and mates and captains on charter boats know how to make good wire leaders. If you can get one of these men to show you how to form and twist the wire leaders you'll soon learn how to make good wire leaders. By following the instructions and drawings given here, however, and with plenty of practice, you can learn how to make neat, secure wire leaders.

The first step when making a single-strand wire leader is to clip off a section of stainless-steel wire. When doing this, you must make allowances for the length of the wire used to form the eyes and the twists. In other words, if you want a wire leader twelve inches long with an eye on each end, you will have to start with a section of wire at least seventeen or eighteen inches long. The longer the end you allow, the easier it will be to work with. Experiment at first to see how long a piece you will need; after that, cut all the wire pieces the same length. Use diagonal pliers to cut the wire into the proper lengths.

To form the eye, grab the wire about two inches from the end with round-nosed pliers (Fig. 151 A) and twist the pliers to the right to form a loop (Fig. 151 B). Next, grab the end of the loop or eye with a pair of flat-nosed pliers (Fig. 151 C). Hold the wire or shift it so that the short end overlaps the main wire on your

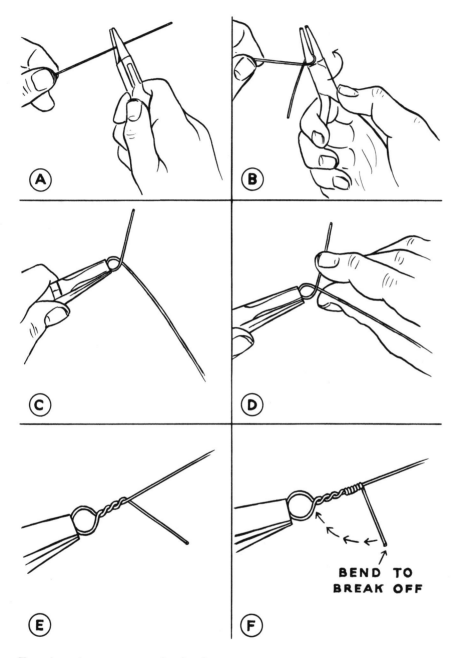

Forming the eye on a wire leader.

Figure 151.

side. Now, using the right thumb and index finger, hold and twist the two wires at the point where they cross to the right (away from you), as shown in Fig. 151 D. Keep twisting the wires so that both of them interlock for several turns (Fig. 151 E). Then make several straight twists of the wire so that it looks as in Fig. 151 F. The remaining short length of wire should be at right angles to the main wire. To break it off, simply bend it sharply toward the eye, then back, then once again, and it will usually break off clean. This is important, because if you use pliers to clip the end off, it will leave a short, sharp stub that can cut your hand when grabbed.

Instead of using pliers to form the eye of the wire leader, you can make up a small, handy jig to do this. Just get a dowel or broomstick handle or similar round wood and cut off about three inches. Then drill a hole in one end so that you can drive in a nail. The thickness of the nail will depend on the size of the eye you want. For small eyes use a thin nail, and for making larger eyes use a thicker-diameter nail. So it's a good idea to make up two or three jigs of various diameters for making different size eyes.

After this center nail is driven or drilled into the wood, take a small screw and screw it next to this nail about $\frac{1}{16}$ inch away. Then to form an eye in the wire, simply place it between the nail and the screw and twist it, as shown in Fig. 152. After you take

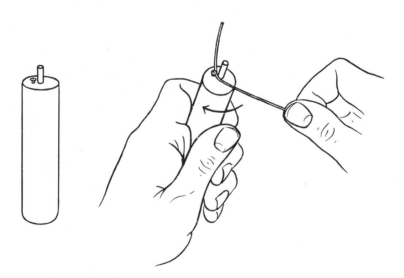

Figure 152.   *Jig for forming wire eyes, and how to use it.*

out the formed eye from the jig, you follow the steps in making the twists as described above.

The other kind of wire used for making leaders is the cable type, which is usually twisted or braided from many fine strands of stainless steel. This cable wire is very flexible and doesn't kink as readily as the single-strand wire. It comes bare or covered with nylon. To use this wire for leaders you need special crimping pliers and brass or copper sleeves, both of which are shown in Fig. 153. To make a loop or eye with this wire, slip the end of the wire through the sleeve until it protrudes about an inch and a half on the other end. Then double the end of the wire back through the sleeve to form the loop or eye, as in Fig. 153. Then the sleeve is

CABLE WIRE LOOP IN SLEEVE

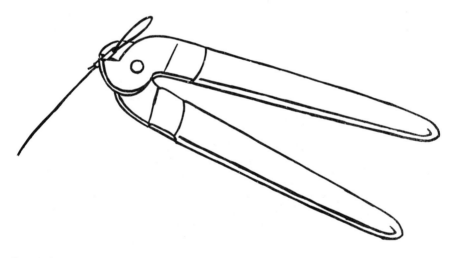

Special crimping pliers for crimping a sleeve. *Figure 153.*

pinched or crimped with the crimping pliers, which flattens it and holds the wire securely. When using nylon-covered cable wire it's a good idea to remove the nylon at the point where the sleeve covers it before crimping. If you want a swivel or snap on the end

of the leader, slip it on the loop or eye before you double the wire
into the sleeve. Such leader-crimping kits with the pliers, sleeves,
and a coil of cable wire can be bought in many fishing-tackle stores
or ordered by mail from one of the suppliers listed in the back
of this book.

Various kinds of snaps, swivels, and other connections are required in both fresh and saltwater fishing. Of course, you can tie
your nylon leaders directly to the lures, and this is most effective
in clear water or when fishing for wary fish. When changing lures,
often, however, this takes up a lot of fishing time, so most anglers
resort to some kind of snap and swivel on the end of the leader.
Such snaps and swivels can be bought in most fishing tackle stores
by the dozen or in larger quantities.

You can also make your own quick-change locking snaps with
little trouble using stainless-steel single-strand wire. Use the finer
wire for freshwater snaps and the heavier gauges for saltwater
snaps. For the freshwater snaps, form them with the small, round-
nosed pliers. Form an eye as described in the section above on making leaders, but slip on a barrel swivel before you close this eye
permanently by making about two or three twists. Next grab the
wire with round-nosed pliers about a half inch or so from the eye.

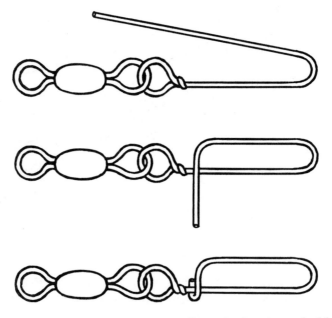

Figure 154.   *Steps in forming a locking snap.*

The actual distance will depend on the size of the snap you are making. Now make a round bend at this point, turning the wire toward the eye you formed. Next, grab the wire again with the pliers near the eye and make a sharp bend to force the wire back toward the twists next to the eye. Finally, take the short end of the wire with pliers and form a catch. In other words, the wire starts from the eye, runs straight for a half inch or so, curves to form a round bend, and then runs back parallel, curves sharply, and meets itself. The drawings in Fig. 154 will show the various steps in forming such snap-swivels.

Snap-swivels in various sizes for fresh and saltwater fishing can be made up in advance, say during the winter months, for the coming fishing season. They are much cheaper than those you buy in a fishing-tackle store and they are just as strong and efficient when properly made. Most important, when you do lose a few or they become old, you can easily replace them with little cost.

15

CARE AND REPAIR
OF FISHING LURES

After the fishing lures are made there is still the problem of taking care of and repairing them so that they will always be in good condition. This requires some effort and time but is usually easy for the angler who makes his own lures. Since he made them and put them together, he also knows how to take them apart and repair them. He also has the tools and fishing-lure parts and materials necessary for such work.

Fishing lures in general do not require much care when storing them in a home or shop. The best idea is to put them into cabinet drawers or individual boxes so that they can be found easily and can be kept dry. In humid climates or near the seashore it is important not to expose the metal parts to the air; otherwise hooks will rust and other metals will corrode. Fishing lures that have feathers or hair should be kept in air-tight containers so that moths and other insects or small animals like mice will not get to them. This also applies to new fishing lures that haven't been used if they have feathers or hair.

Lures that have been used require considerable care if you want to get the maximum use from them. Freshwater plugs usually require less care and repair than saltwater ones. But any plug that is chipped, cracked or battered can quickly be made to look like new.

Plugs that are slightly chipped can be merely touched up with a small brush, using enamels or lacquers. But if the wooden body is badly cracked or the paint has peeled off, it should be given a complete paint job. Here too, you can use a brush to paint the entire plug with enamel or lacquer. But you'll do it quicker and get a nicer finish if you use a spray can or spray gun. If you use a brush and enamel paint you do not have to remove the hooks unless you want to replace them with new ones. First sandpaper the plug, then paint it with white enamel. Two or three coats may be necessary to cover it completely. Then add the other colors. If you use a spray can or gun and fast-drying lacquer or enamel, remove the hooks for best results. Sandpaper the old paint if the plug is not too badly cracked. If it is badly chipped and cracked you can do a better job if you dip the plug body in paint remover and then scrape off the old paint or lacquer. After this, you can proceed to spray the wooden plug body the same way as if it were a new plug just being made. When the paint job is finished, replace the old hooks or add new ones.

The hooks on a plug, especially if it is a saltwater type, should be examined closely. If they are only slightly rusted they can be cleaned with steel wool or emery cloth, then wiped with an oily rag. You can also varnish or paint the hooks with black enamel or lacquer to protect them from rust for longer periods.

If the hooks are badly rusted, however, they should be replaced with new ones. When doing this it is important to use the same size and weight as the old ones in order that the action of the plug is not changed in any way. It's always a good idea to check the points and barbs of old or new hooks to make sure they are sharp and not bent or broken. A few minutes spent with a small file or Carborundum sharpening stone will pay dividends later on when a fish with a tough mouth strikes and is hooked.

Wood or cork spin bugs should be checked to see if the hair or feathers are in good shape and not thinned out or chewed up too much. If this is the case, the best idea is to remove the old hair and add new material. After the hair or feathers have been tied or glued on, the bug can be repainted with enamel or lacquer using a small brush.

Spoons and spinners should be wiped dry after using to prevent them from tarnishing or corroding. If they were used in salt water, it's a good idea to rinse them in fresh water, then wipe them dry before storing them away. You can also wipe the spoon, hooks, and connections with an oily rag to keep them in good condition. If the spoons or spinners are tarnished, they can usually be polished with metal polish.

After spoons and spinners become badly chipped or corroded they can often be replated if you have saved enough of them to make it worthwhile. Or you can take a few of the spoons or spinners and spray them or paint them white, yellow, or silver. Of course, if you make your own spinners you can always make up new blades or spoon bodies or order them from the mail-order houses and replace the old blades.

With jigs you have to watch the hook and the hair, feather, or nylon skirts. If the hook is badly rusted and weakened, the best thing to do is to discard it and put it aside until the time comes to make new jigs when you can remelt the old ones. If, however, the hook is in good condition but the hair has thinned out or shredded, you can remove it and tie on new hair, feathers, or nylon. If the jig is painted, it can be rubbed with steel wool or sandpaper and then repainted or resprayed.

Metal squids should also be examined to see if they require work. Usually all you need to do is to take some steel wool or metal polish and rub the squid to bring out the shine. If the feathers have been thinned out or if they are chewed up, remove them and tie on new ones. A metal squid need not be recast unless the point or barb of the hook is broken or the hook is badly rusted and weak. Then you can melt it and pour new squids. Such squids usually contain some lead, so do not add any more of this metal. You can, however, add some additional block tin if you have it. This tin and lead can be used over and over as often as required. That's another big advantage in making your own metal squids: you don't have to use such lures if the hooks become badly rusted or the metal squid gets banged up and dented. Merely save them and then pour new metal squids.

Rigged eels and eelskin lures are highly perishable and must be kept frozen or in salt brine or some other preservative when not in use. Before being used, rigged eels and eelskin lures should be examined carefully to see that they are not torn. Rigged eels tend to get soft after being used for any length of time. Then they start falling apart and are not much use. There isn't much you can do to prevent this from happening except to keep them in salt brine when you are not using them. Once an eel starts to fall apart or gets too soft you might as well as discard it and use a fresh one. Of course, you can salvage the hooks or swivels to use when rigging fresh eels. Eelskin lures are pretty durable, but when the skin gets too old it can be taken off and a new one can be tied in its place. Here too, you should watch the hooks and wire or chain to make certain they are not weakened and still in good condition.

When it comes to the plastic worms, plastic eels, and other plastic lures that are soft, you have to make a lot of replacements, because they do not stand up too well and are easily ripped or bitten up by fish. If you make a lot of plastic worms or baits, you can always rig them with new hooks or old hooks and throw away or save the old worms for remelting. Plastic eels used in salt water or any other plastic lures made of soft material used in salt water don't last too long if you catch such fish with sharp teeth as bluefish, king mackerel, barracuda, or sharks. Here again, it pays to carry plenty of spares and replace those which have been chopped off or slashed too badly.

The more rigid plastic tube lures or rubber tube lures are tougher and stand up much better and longer in salt water. The hook is the weakest link, if it rusts and has to be replaced or if you have to use a new tube lure. If you do catch many fish with sharp teeth on the same lure, it may get slashed or chopped up and then has to be replaced with a new one.

When it comes to leaders and connections it is very important to use only the strongest. If you suspect any weakness it's a good idea to discard that leader and tie or make up a new one. Nylon leader material or fishing line is inexpensive, and if your leaders are frayed or nicked or weakened they should be thrown away. Single-strand wire leaders tend to kink, and if they have too sharp a bend that cannot be straightened out, they should be thrown away and new ones made. You should also check the eyes or loops on wire leaders to make sure they haven't slipped or closed. An eye that is closed too much on a wire leader can kill the action of a lure. Snaps and swivels that have been used too long and too often should also be replaced with new ones.

In general, when examining any fishing lure you have made, it's wise to repair it if you have the least doubt about its condition. If it cannot be repaired, throw it away after saving the usable parts. It doesn't pay to take chances with a fishing lure that is weak or too old. You may hook a record fish and lose it if the lure is not dependable. Many anglers who buy their fishing lures in tackle stores often use them until they fall apart before buying new ones. But if you make your own fishing lures you can afford to use only those which are in good condition.

APPENDIX

MAIL-ORDER HOUSES THAT SELL FISHING-LURE PARTS

Most of the firms listed below sell fishing tackle, fly-tying materials, fishing-lure parts, hardware, hooks, feathers, and hair that can be used to make fishing lures. Before ordering such materials, write for the catalogue.

Herter's Inc.
Highway 13 South
Waseca, Minn. 56093

Midland Tackle Co.
66 Route 17
Sloatsburg, N. Y. 10974

Finnysports
2910 Glanzman Rd.
Toledo, Ohio 43614

Limit Manufacturing Corp.
515 Melody Lane
Richardson, Texas 75080

Carolina Novelty Co.
2412 Kenmore Ave.
Charlotte, N. C. 28204

The Netcraft Co.
3101 Sylvania Ave.
Toledo, Ohio 43613

Cole, Dominick & Rogg, Inc.
52 West 52nd St.
New York, N. Y. 10020
(Surgical tubes and plastic tubes)

Reed Tackle
Box 390
Caldwell, N. J. 07006

E. Hille
P. O. Box 269
Williamsport, Penna. 17701

INDEX